trash to treasure

Unleash your creative spirit with dozens of stylish, innovative projects — all made with materials you already have at home! Turn paper towel rolls into an elegant pillared picture frame. Convert an old pair of overalls into a clever travel organizer for the kids. Transform a worn-out wicker basket into a beribboned memo board. It's easier than you might think! Our simple instructions, precise diagrams and patterns, and full-color photographs will help you create confidently — no matter what your skill level. Choose from more than 75 projects in five fabulous sections! **Simply Inspired** is chock-full of jewelry, accessories, and other small projects that are ideal for everyday use. Get in on the scrapbooking trend with **Memorable Papers**, a section devoted to paper goods and gifts. Don't clean out the attic just yet — **Hidden Treasures** will reveal concealed potential in objects you thought you'd never use again. Consult **Home Style** for striking accents you can use throughout the house, or browse through **Garden Fresh** for delightful porch and yard décor. So turn the page and starting turning your "trash" to treasure!

LEISURE ARTS, INC.
Little Rock, Arkansas

editorial staff

Vice President and Editor-in-Chief:
  Sandra Graham Case
Executive Director of Publications:
  Cheryl Nodine Gunnells
Senior Publications Director: Susan White Sullivan
Director of Designer Relations: Debra Nettles
Design Director: Cyndi Hansen
Editorial Director: Susan Frantz Wiles
Publications Director: Kristine Anderson Mertes
Art Operations Director: Jeff Curtis
Director of Public Relations and Retail Marketing:
  Stephen Wilson

DESIGN

Design Manager: Diana Sanders Cates
Design Captains: Cherece Athy,
  Polly Tullis Browning, and
  Peggy Elliott Cunningham
Designers: Tonya Bates, Kim Kern,
  Anne Pulliam Stocks, and Becky Werle
Design Assistant: Lucy Combs Beaudry
Production Assistant: Karla Edgar

TECHNICAL

Technical Editor: Leslie Schick Gorrell

Book Coordinator and Senior Technical Writer:
  Theresa Hicks Young
Technical Writer: Shawnna B. Bowles

EDITORIAL

Managing Editor: Alan Caudle
Associate Editor: Kimberly L. Ross

ART

Art Publications Director: Rhonda Hodge Shelby
Art Imaging Director: Mark Hawkins
Art Category Manager: Lora Puls
Lead Graphic Artist: Dayle S. Carozza
Graphic Artists: Chad Brown, Amy Gerke,
  Stephanie Hamling, Brittany Skarda, and
  Elaine Wheat
Imaging Technicians: Stephanie Johnson and
  Mark Potter
Staff Photographer: Russ Ganser
Photography Stylist: Janna Laughlin
Publishing Systems Administrator: Becky Riddle
Publishing Systems Assistants: Clint Hanson,
  John Rose, and Chris Wertenberger

business staff

Publisher: Rick Barton
Vice President, Finance: Tom Siebenmorgen
Director of Corporate Planning and Development:
  Laticia Mull Dittrich
Vice President, Retail Marketing: Bob Humphrey
Vice President, Sales: Ray Shelgosh
Vice President, National Accounts: Pam Stebbins

Director of Sales and Services: Margaret Reinold
Vice President, Operations: Jim Dittrich
Comptroller, Operations: Rob Thieme
Retail Customer Service Manager: Stan Raynor
Print Production Manager: Fred F. Pruss

Made in the United States of America.

Library of Congress Catalog Number 98-65089
International Standard Book Number 1-57486-320-7

10 9 8 7 6 5 4 3 2 1

simply inspired

From jewelry to accessories, you'll love these imaginative ideas for practical living. Turn a colorful shower curtain and an ice cream bucket into a handy carry-all. Change cast-off clothing into a checkbook set or a beaded bracelet. Transform a plastic twist-tie into a fanciful bookmark ... or gum wrappers into a starry pendant. How original!

*imaginative
ideas for
practical
living*

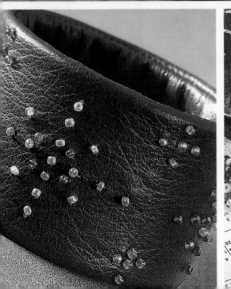

puzzling jewelry

Mischievous shapes combine with fashionable colors and textures for a chic new look. These distinctive accessories provide a challenging use for old puzzle pieces.

1. Use the paint pen to outline the front of each puzzle piece; paint the backs and sides with acrylic paint. Apply sealer to the front and back of each piece.

2. Punch a hole in the desired number of puzzle pieces. Follow the manufacturer's instructions to attach an eyelet and a jump ring in each hole. (The teal beaded necklace and the earrings do not have jump rings.)

3. For a necklace, thread beads and puzzle pieces onto silk cord (knot the ends together) or a chain.

4. For a bracelet, thread beads and puzzle pieces onto a length of clear stretch cord long enough to slide over your hand; knot the ends together.

5. For each earring, thread a puzzle piece onto the center of a 4" length of wire. Twist the wire tightly around itself several times to secure the puzzle piece. Thread beads onto the twisted wire, then twist one end of the wire tightly around itself to secure the beads; trim the wire end. Thread the remaining wire end through the attachment ring on the earring post; twist wire back around itself to secure in place. Glue a bead onto the post front.

Tip:
Use fray preventative or glue on the ends of the silk cord to keep it from fraying.

Recycled items:
• small cardboard puzzle pieces
• beads
• necklace chain (optional)

You'll also need:
• gold paint pen
• gold acrylic paint
• paintbrushes
• clear acrylic sealer
• 1/8" dia. hole punch
• 1/8" dia. eyelets and a setter
• jewelry jump rings
• #6 silk bead cord
• clear jewelry stretch cord
• jewelry wire
• earring posts with attachment loops
• clear-drying jewelry glue

fanciful wire bookmarks

Treat your favorite bookworm to a whimsical page keeper made of plastic-coated twist-ties. Zigzag patterns and colorful beads or charms make these bookmarks extra-special.

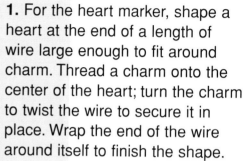

1. For the heart marker, shape a heart at the end of a length of wire large enough to fit around charm. Thread a charm onto the center of the heart; turn the charm to twist the wire to secure it in place. Wrap the end of the wire around itself to finish the shape.

2. For the name marker, thread desired beads onto the end of a length of wire. Wrap the end of the wire around itself, forming a loop.

3. Thread desired beads onto the wire covering the wrapped end and knot the wire below the beads.

4. Form bends in the remainder of the wire, then curl the end to finish.

Recycled items:
- long plastic-coated wire twist-ties
- assorted charms and beads

Tip:
Many toys and appliances are secured in their packaging with plastic-coated twist-ties.

wineglass markers

Charming wineglass markers are a unique solution to the "which glass is mine?" dilemma. For a special touch, use shapes or colors that coordinate with your party theme.

1. For each marker, thread a bead onto a 5" length of twist-tie. Curl the wire on each side of the bead.

2. Twist the ends of the tie together to secure the marker around the stem of a glass.

Recycled items:
- colorful beads
- plastic-coated wire twist-ties

Display eight photos in the space of two with our "high-rise" frame. Buttons, beads, and wire give this tower of hinged jewelry boxes a contemporary flair.

memory tower

1. Open each box and remove any liners.

2. For each box, cut a piece of the paper bag large enough to cover the outside of the box and wrap to the inside; cut another piece of paper to cover the inside hinge. Crumple, then smooth the paper pieces; glue the pieces to the box. *Dry Brush* the box brown, then highlight with rub-on finish.

3. Stack and glue the boxes together.

4. For each bead finial, thread a button (for the base) and assorted beads onto a length of wire. Make a spiral at the top end of the wire, then coil the bottom end flat against the base. Glue each finial in place.

5. For a topper, thread several beads onto a long length of wire; twist and curl the wire to hold the beads in place, then glue the wire along the top of the frame.

6. Cut photos to fit inside each frame, then spot glue them in place.

Tip:
Use clothespins to hold objects in place until the glue dries.

Recycled items:
- hinged jewelry boxes in graduated sizes that are styled alike and open at the same angle
- brown paper bags
- assorted buttons and beads
- photographs

You'll also need:
- tacky glue
- brown acrylic paint
- paintbrushes
- gold metallic rub-on finish
- craft wire

Crafting Technique:
- *Dry Brush*, page 158

Button and Bead Bracelet

1. Leaving 2" on each end of the twist-tie, thread buttons and beads onto a tie long enough to slide over your hand onto your wrist.

2. Thread the twist-tie ends together through another bead and pull taut; add a charm, then twist the wire around itself to secure. Glue a bead over the twisted wire, then trim the ends.

Recycled Items:
• long plastic-coated twist-ties
• buttons and beads
• metal charm

You'll also need
• craft glue

Tip:
Many toys and appliances are secured in their packaging with plastic-coated twist-ties.

Leather Bracelet

1. Cut a 1³/₄" wide strip from the plastic bottle long enough to fit loosely around your wrist with a ³/₄" overlap; round the corners.

2. Draw around the plastic strip two times on the wrong side of the leather; cut out the leather strips ¹/₄" outside the drawn lines.

3. Trace the beading pattern from page 149 onto tracing paper. Spacing and repeating pattern as necessary, transfer the design onto the right side of one leather strip. Knotting each bead individually in place, use clear thread to sew the beads onto the leather.

4. Matching right sides, leaving one end open for inserting the plastic strip, and sewing ¹/₈" outside the drawn lines, sew the leather strips together. Turn the cover right-side out and insert the plastic strip; sew the opening closed.

5. Align snaps between the ends of the bracelet, then sew them in place.

Recycled Items:
• 20-oz. plastic beverage bottle
• soft and flexible leather pieces

You'll also need:
• tracing paper
• transfer paper
• clear nylon thread
• seed beads
• sew-on snaps

beaded
bracelets

Earthy beaded bracelets are all the rage and guaranteed to add a trendy touch to any outfit. The leather cuff is crafted from a surprising resource, and the slide makes sophisticated use of old buttons and beads.

candy
canister

Dressed up with pretty papers and trim, an empty coffee creamer can becomes an ornamental dispenser for sweet treats. Display on the coffee table so guests can indulge, or present as a thoughtful gift.

1. Keeping the canister closed, apply primer, then paint to the top of the canister.

2. Cover the canister with textured paper.

3. Cut three 2" x 3" rectangles from scrapbooking paper; then stamp a design at the center of each rectangle. Glue the rectangles to the can. For frames, cut strips from the edges of the sheets of stickers and adhere them around the rectangles.

4. Glue lengths of ribbon and trim around the top and bottom of the can. Tie a length of ribbon into a bow and glue to the top of the can.

Recycled items:
- coffee creamer canister
- sheets of self-adhesive stickers
- remnants of ribbons and trim

You'll also need:
- acrylic primer
- spray paint
- craft glue
- textured and scrapbooking paper
- rubber stamp and ink pad

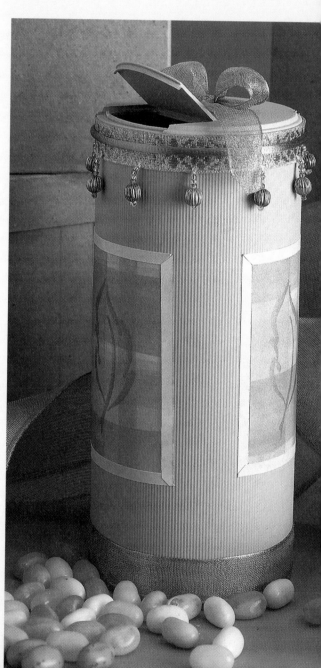

stellar pendant

For a one-of-a-kind accessory, personalize a sparkly star with jewels and beads. This foil-covered pendant looks divine worn as a shimmering brooch or a dazzling necklace.

Recycled items:
- foil gum wrappers
- charm
- necklace chain

You'll also need:
- craft glue
- 3¼" wide wooden star cutout
- black acrylic paint
- paintbrushes
- micro-beads
- acrylic jewels
- colored craft wire
- pin clasp

1. Crumple gum wrappers, then smooth them out. Overlapping wrappers to cover completely, glue wrappers onto the sides and front of the star.

2. Paint the star black; use a soft cloth to wipe away excess paint.

3. Embellish the star with the charm, micro-beads, and acrylic jewels. Wrap and coil craft wire around the star and glue to secure.

4. Glue the pin clasp to the back of the star. For a necklace, use the pin clasp to hang the star from a chain.

A vibrant bath caddy is just right for keeping beauty essentials organized. Ideal for a dorm or shared apartment, this dressed-up ice cream bucket could also store art supplies, note cards, photos, and more.

clever
carry-all

Recycled items:
- solid-colored plastic shower liner curtain
- 1-gal. plastic ice cream bucket
- plastic shower curtain with motifs
- small cord and gimp pieces

You'll also need:
- clear-drying silicone adhesive

1. Trimming to fit and folding the edge down over the bottom, use a piece of the shower liner to cover the outside of the bucket. Draw around the bucket on the liner; cut out the piece just inside the drawn line and adhere to the bottom of the bucket.

2. Cut motifs from the shower curtain. Overlapping their edges, adhere the motifs around the bucket.

3. Punch holes in the bucket where the original handle was attached.

4. For the braided handle, cut three lengths of cord and three lengths of gimp twice as long as you want the finished handle to be. Knot one end of the cord and gimp lengths together, then thread through one hole, catching the knot on the outside of the bucket. Braid the handle, then thread the end through the remaining hole and knot. Fray the ends of the handle.

1. Leaving 4" between drawings, draw around the bottom of the box two times on the wrong side of a piece of fabric; cut out pieces 2" outside drawn lines. Clipping as necessary and folding edges to sides or insides of box, glue pieces to the lid and the outside bottom of the box.

2. Measure around the box; add 1¹/₂". Measure height of box; add 1". Cut a strip of fabric the determined measurements. Press each end, then long edges of strip ¹/₂" to the wrong side. Overlapping ends at back, glue strip around the box.

3. Referring to Fig 1, make holes in the box for handle (A), clasp (B), clasp bead (C), and dangle (D).

Fig. 1

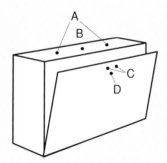

4. For the handle, thread beads onto a length of wire, then insert the wire ends through the handle holes (A). Bend, then hot glue the wires on the inside of the box to secure in place.

5. For the clasp, push the metal part of the ponytail holder through the clasp hole (B), then sew a large bead to the box (C). Thread several beads onto floss and insert the floss end through the dangle hole (D); knot the floss several times on the inside of the box, then dab with hot glue to secure. Attach a decorative earring or charm to the end of the dangle.

6. Cover the inside of the box with felt or fabric.

Recycled items:
- cardboard cigar box
- fabric remnants
- beads
- small elastic ponytail holder
- earring or charm
- felt remnants (optional)

You'll also need:
- tacky glue
- heavy-duty craft wire
- hot glue gun
- embroidery floss

retro handbag

Go retro with this pretty pastel pocketbook. The boxy shape and patterned fabric are reminiscent of the Sixties, while the soft colors create a fun, feminine air.

Paying bills is a little less dreary with this cheerful checkbook cover made of felted wool. Adorn with a floral appliqué and pair with a rainbow-beaded ink pen. Your finances are looking more attractive already!

felted wool
checkbook set

1. Cut a 10" x 18" piece from wool garment. Using a long kitchen utensil to hold the wool piece completely under water, boil the wool piece for twenty minutes…this creates a very tightly-woven felt-like fabric called felted wool. Remove the wool from the water and dry it thoroughly. With an iron set to wool, press the piece.

2. Cut a $6\frac{1}{2}$" x $12\frac{3}{4}$" cover piece and two $\frac{1}{2}$" x 3" strips from the felted wool.

3. Using three strands of floss, work *Blanket Stitches* along the short edges of the cover piece and the long edges of the strips. Fold each short edge of the cover piece 3" to the inside. Referring to Fig. 1, cut $\frac{1}{2}$" long slits along folds of cover.

Fig. 1

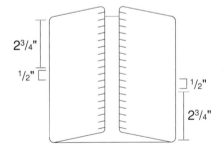

4. Fold the strips in half, then sew the ends of each strip together to form a loop. Insert $\frac{1}{2}$" of the loops into the slits and pin them in place.

5. Using three strands of floss, work *Blanket Stitches* along the edges of the cover.

6. Trace the flower and leaf patterns, page 155, onto tracing paper. Using the patterns, cut one flower from yellow felt and three leaves from green felt.

7. Sew the flowers and leaves, then a cluster of seed beads for the flower center, onto the front cover…be careful not to sew through the inside layer of the cover.

8. For the beaded pen, cover the pen with tape, then roll the pen in micro and seed beads.

Recycled items:
• wool garment

You'll also need
• coordinating embroidery floss
• tracing paper
• yellow and green felt
• seed and micro beads
• stick ink pen
• double-stick tape

Crafting Technique:
• *Blanket Stitches*, page 159

novel
purse

Fashioned from a sturdy hardback book, this witty handbag is an amusing accessory for a student or a scholar. The delightful "literary work" flaunts a dainty shoulder strap made from decorative trim and a distinctive button embellishment.

1. For the liner, draw around the open book on the wrong side of the fabric; extend one end of the rectangle 3". Cut out the piece ¹/₄" outside the drawn lines. Repeat the step to cut out a second fabric piece.

2. Pin the pieces right sides together. Referring to Fig. 1, mark the extended end, then trim the corners ¹/₄" outside the marked lines. Leaving an opening for turning, sew the pieces together along the drawn lines. Clip the corners and turn the liner right-side out. Press the liner, then topstitch along the edges.

Fig. 1

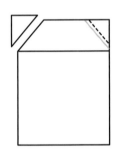

3. For the side gussets, add 2" to the width of the book front cover…spine to opening edge. Determine how wide you want the purse to open and add 1". Cut two pieces of fabric the determined measurements.

4. Press one short edge of each piece ¹/₂" to the wrong side. Press ¹/₂" to the wrong side again and topstitch in place. Referring to Fig. 2, glue ¹/₂" of the side edges of the gussets to the book cover.

Fig. 2

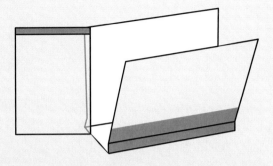

5. Gathering as necessary, glue the bottom edge of the gussets to the spine. For the handle, glue the ends of the trim to the inside back cover.

6. Matching the straight end of the liner with the edge of the front cover, glue the liner in the purse. Glue the fastener between the flap and the front of the purse. Attach a button to the front of the flap.

Recycled items:
- hardcover book with pages removed (we used a 5¹/₂" x 7¹/₂" book with a 1¹/₂" spine)
- fabric scraps to coordinate with book cover
- length of decorative trim for the handle
- button

You'll also need:
- fabric glue
- hook and loop fastener dots

overall
travel organizer

1. Use the seam ripper to separate the front and back pieces of the overalls at the side and inner leg seams. Cut the shoulder straps from the overalls. Matching right sides and side edges, fold each piece in half lengthwise. Continuing from the bottom of the center seam, sew a straight line down the inner legs on each piece, then trim the seams to ½".

2. Cut straight across the back piece 3" above the pockets and just below the bottom of the ruler pocket (the piece should be about 13" tall). Press the top edge ½" to the wrong side, then ½" to the wrong side again; topstitch in place. Fuse a length of ribbon along the top edge.

3. Fuse lengths of ribbon across the pockets and along the waistband under the belt loops, if applicable.

4. Pin the pocket piece to the front piece just below the side seams of the front pockets. Cut the bottom and side edges even; remove the pocket piece.

5. Working under the side pockets and below the waistband, fuse a piece of interfacing to the back side of the front piece. Sew the side pockets in place along the bottom edges.

6. Matching the right side of the pocket piece and the wrong side of the front piece, pin, then sew the pieces together along the side and bottom edges. Clip the corners and turn the pocket piece to the front.

7. Matching right sides and raw edges, sew the straps together across the raw edges. Hook the strap to the organizer, then secure the strap around the headrest of the car seat.

> *Tip:*
> To keep the organizer against the seat, thread a long length of ribbon through one buttonhole in the organizer, around the seat, through the buttonhole on the other side of the organizer, then tie the ends into a bow!

Recycled items:
• child-sized denim overalls
• ribbon

You'll also need:
• seam ripper
• ½" wide fusible web tape
• heavy-duty fusible interfacing

You can have peace of mind during road trips, thanks to our overall organizer. Filled with a variety of toys and games, this handy bag can keep kids happy and busy for hours.

trinket frame

Childhood toys make a simple frame and mat much more memorable. Choose old favorites lately discarded or scour garage sales and flea markets for trinkets that reflect youngsters' interests.

Tip:
If you don't have mats the correct size, you can cut them from cardboard!

Allow primer, paint, and adhesives to dry after each application.

1. Apply primer, then paint to the frame.

2. Overlapping edges and wrapping to the back, glue the money randomly onto the mat.

3. Secure the mat in the frame, then use silicone adhesive to secure the toys and trinkets to the mat as desired.

Recycled items:
• wooden picture frame with mat(s)
• play paper money
• small toys and trinkets

You'll also need:
• acrylic primer
• paintbrushes
• acrylic paint
• craft glue
• clear-drying silicone adhesive

coaster
flashcards

1. Apply primer to each coaster, then paint them different colors. Cut a piece of card stock to fit in the center of each coaster; glue it in place.

2. Cover the container with card stock. Paint stripes on the container; outline the stripes with the pen.

3. *Découpage* pictures from the books and magazines onto the card stock circles and the container.

4. For the handle, hot glue the ends of a length of cord down the sides of the container.

Crafting Technique:
• Découpage, page 157

Teach children that learning is fun with this sturdy educational game. Coaster "flashcards" help tots practice the names of colors and objects, while a cast-off canister keeps the pieces together when they're not in use.

Recycled items:
• wooden coasters with cork centers
• cardboard canister with lid to accommodate coasters
• children's books and activity magazines
• scraps of cord

You'll also need:
• white acrylic primer
• paintbrushes
• assorted acrylic paint
• white card stock
• découpage glue
• paint pen
• hot glue gun

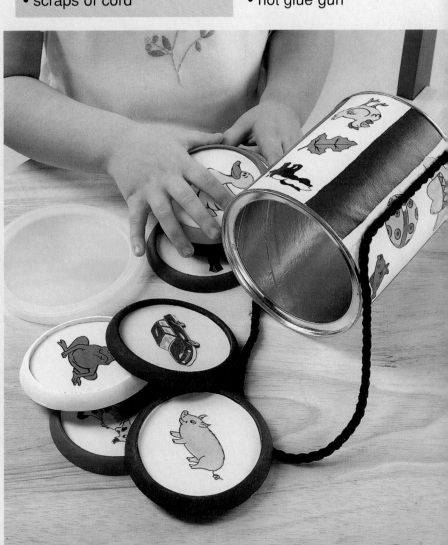

Show off favorite photos and other tiny treasures "scrapbook-style" in a dressy baby collage. This creative hanger frame is sure to spark lots of "baby talk."

FEEDS SELF

EATS FINGERFOOD

POINTS TO EYES

PLAYS "PAT-A-CAKE"

BABY LAURA

dressed-up
baby frame

1. For the background, draw around the hanger onto scrapbook paper and cardboard. Cut out the pieces just inside the drawn lines; glue the pieces together.

2. For each frame, draw around a photo on the wrong side of a coordinating sheet of paper. Cut out the frame opening $1/4$" inside the drawn lines; determine the width for the frame, then use craft scissors to cut out the frame. Arrange and glue the photos and frames onto the background.

3. Stamp the baby's name onto scrapbook paper; use craft scissors to cut out the nameplate.

4. Glue the background to the hanger. Decorate the frame with the nameplate, stickers, decorative buttons, and a ribbon bow.

Recycled items:
- child-size plastic clothes hanger
- lightweight cardboard (we used a shirt box)
- photographs
- leftover stickers from a baby calendar
- decorative buttons
- ribbon

You'll also need:
- scrapbook papers
- tacky glue
- decorative-edge craft scissors
- alphabet rubber stamps and ink pad

Tip:
Make reduced photocopies of baby's footprints from the hospital to use as accents!

froggy
toy tote

Adorable "froggy" fabric transforms a disposable wipes container into a portable toy box. The friendly amphibian is just right for storing stuffed animals and other childish knickknacks until playtime.

Recycled items:
- plastic diaper wipes box
- foam mouse pad
- cloth belt

You'll also need:
- fabric to cover the box
- fabric glue
- jumbo rickrack
- heavy-weight fusible interfacing
- tracing paper
- poster board
- acrylic paint
- paintbrushes
- paint pen
- awl
- two brass paper fasteners

1. Measure around box; add $1/2$". Measure height of box from under rim to bottom of box; add $1/2$". Cut a strip of fabric the determined measurements. Starting at one side of box, glue fabric strip around box, gathering fabric at corners to fit. Glue rickrack down corners of box.

2. Draw around the lid on the wrong side of fabric; cut out 1" outside drawn lines. Wrapping edges to the underside of lid and trimming around the pop-up hole, glue the fabric piece to the lid. Draw around pop-up lid (including front lip and back hinge) on wrong side of fabric. Fuse fabric to wrong side of another piece of fabric, then cut out $1/4$" outside drawn line. Glue fabric piece to pop-up lid. Glue rickrack along lip, hinge, and edges of lid.

3. Trace the eye pattern from page 149 onto tracing paper and cut out. Use the pattern to cut two eye shapes from the mouse pad. Draw around pattern four times on the wrong side of fabric and twice on poster board; cut out two fabric pieces 1" outside drawn lines, two fabric pieces $1/2$" outside drawn lines, and poster board pieces along drawn lines. For each eye, use the larger fabric piece to cover the mouse pad eye, wrapping and gluing the fabric edges to the back. Cover the poster board eye with the remaining fabric piece, then matching wrong sides, glue it to the back of the mouse pad eye.

4. Paint eyes and details on the face; use the paint pen to outline the painted areas. Glue eyes to the pop-up lid.

5. Cut the belt to the desired length for a handle, allowing for extra length to go down sides of box and wrap to bottom. Measure around belt; add $1/2$". Cut a piece of fabric the length of belt piece by determined measurement. Press one long edge $1/4$" to wrong side. Placing raw edge along center of belt, glue fabric piece around belt. Starting with ends at bottom of box, glue ends of the handle to sides of box.

6. Use an awl to poke a hole through the handle on each side of the box just under the rim. Insert a paper fastener through each hole and spread the prongs to secure the handle.

7. Draw around the bottom of the box on poster board and the wrong side of fabric; cut the poster board $1/4$" inside the drawn lines and the fabric $1/2$" outside drawn lines. Wrap and glue the fabric around the poster board. Glue the fabric-covered poster board piece to the bottom of the box, covering the rickrack and handle ends.

Tip:
If you cannot find frog fabric or want to make something other than a frog, it's easy! Pick fabric and paint colors for another animal instead...the eyes will work for any critter!

friendship frame

1. Cut away the toes and cuffs from the socks; cut the remaining parts into $1/2$"w loops. Weave the loops into the desired pattern on the loom.

2. For the stand, cut a 2" x 7" piece of cardboard. Score the strip $1/2$" from the top edge and punch a hole near each top corner; turn the strip over and score $2^1/2$" from the bottom edge (Fig. 1). Glue bottom edge to bottom of the loom, then tack the top edge of the stand to back of weaving through the holes.

Fig. 1

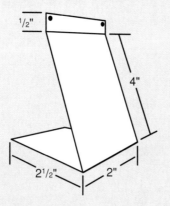

3. Glue a square photo onto a piece of card stock, then use craft scissors to cut around the photo. Center and tape the photo to the front side of the weaving.

4. Cut a square from plastic $3/4$" larger on each side than the photo frame. Using floss, sew one button to each corner of the plastic through the weaving.

5. Glue beads to the front of the frame to spell out a message or a name.

Recycled items:
- socks
- potholder weaving loom
- cardboard back of a writing tablet
- photograph
- clear plastic take-out container
- buttons

You'll also need:
- craft knife and cutting mat
- $1/16$" dia. hole punch
- tacky glue
- embroidery floss
- card stock
- decorative-edge craft scissors
- double-stick tape
- alphabet beads

Jazz up a playroom with a lively frame transformed from the ever-popular childhood potholder loom. Bright colors and big buttons will make this cheery display a natural favorite for all ages.

memorable
papers

With a little ingenuity, ordinary throwaways can become pages and pages of tokens and trinkets. Decorate a charming postcard set with an adorable mouse-pad stamp. Alter a book into a special keepsake or dress up manila-folder place cards with fancy tissue paper. Craft a pocket journal from cardboard and gift wrap. Delightful!

pages and
pages of
tokens and
trinkets

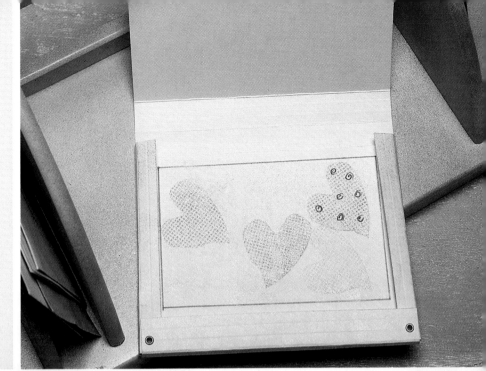

special thoughts
keepsake

1. Draw a heart on the first page of the book. Use a craft knife to cut through several pages at a time until the heart is cut out about 1/4" deep.

2. Apply rub-on finish to the inside edges of the cutout. Cut a piece from the gift bag, larger than the cutout; glue it to the page behind the cutout. Thread a piece of ribbon through a heart pendant and tape the ends to an inner page so that the pendant hangs in the opening.

3. Use the ink pad to lightly stamp the inside cover and first page of the book green.

4. Apply tape about 1/4" from the edges of the cover and first page. Follow manufacturer's instructions to apply crafting foil to the tape strips.

5. Use craft scissors to cut out a message and words of endearment from the cards. Lightly rub chalk across the cutouts for an aged look. Use the ink pad to stamp the edges of the cutouts and the pages gold. Following manufacturer's instructions, use eyelets to attach the message to the first page.

6. Poke a hole through all the pages at the center side edge. Glue the earring in the hole, then trim the post. Glue the last page of the book to the inside back cover.

7. Shaping coils in one end of each wire, bend, twist, and coil three lengths of wire. Arrange the wires on the inside front cover and glue the large pendant over the ends. Place the word cutouts in the wire coils.

Recycled items:
- hard bound book the desired size for frame
- coordinating gift bag
- narrow sheer ribbon
- heart pendant, dangle post-style earring, and large pendant
- greeting cards

You'll also need:
- craft knife
- gold rub-on finish
- clear-drying silicone adhesive
- double-sided tape
- green and gold ink pads
- gold crafting foil
- decorative-edge craft scissors
- brown chalk
- small eyelets and eyelet tool kit
- copper craft wire

Altered books are the latest trend! Adorn yours with bits of jewelry and endearing sentiments to create a sweet memento for someone special.

Warmest Wishes

Special thoughts

Thinking of you

Whatever makes you happy,
whatever makes you smile,
Whatever lifts your spirits
and makes your day worthwhile,
Whatever brings you laughter
and helps your dreams come true—
That's exactly what we're wishing
with pride and love for you.

stylish album

Use craft glue for all gluing unless otherwise indicated.

1. Using paper egg cartons to make the pulp, follow *Making Handmade Paper* to make enough paper clay to fill the wrong side of the lid.

2. To make the front cover plaque, press clay into the lid. Smooth a layer of cheesecloth over the mixture in the lid, then add another layer of clay mixture. (The center of the plaque should be about ¼" thick and smooth.) Allow the plaque to dry overnight.

3. Remove the plaque from the lid and allow it to dry completely. Paint the plaque tan.

4. Cut four 1" wide strips the lengths of the sides of the binder and a 1" x 4" length from the paper bag. Fold and glue the long edges of each strip ¼" to the back.

5. Alternating metallic paint colors, *Sponge Paint* the plaque and the fronts of the strips. Follow the manufacturer's instructions to add gold leaf, then antiquing glaze to the strips. Set the 4" strip aside. Tear a piece of wallpaper to fit on the plaque and apply antiquing glaze to the edges.

6. Cover the outside of the binder with wallpaper. Glue the torn paper piece to the plaque, then glue the plaque to the binder.

7. Miter the ends of the long strips and glue them along the front edges of the binder.

8. Fold the ends of a 5" length of ribbon ½" to the back. Glue the tassel to the bottom of the ribbon, then glue the 4" paper strip around the bottom of the ribbon, trimming ends if necessary. Write the year on the ribbon, then glue the top edge of the ribbon and a button to the plaque.

Crafting Techniques:
• *Making Handmade Paper*, page 52
• *Sponge Painting*, page 158

Recycled items:

- paper egg cartons
- decorative plastic container lid suitable as a mold for a plaque
- ring binder
- brown paper bag
- wallpaper pieces
- wire-edged sheer metallic ribbon
- small tassel
- button

You'll be proud to display your cherished memories inside our elegant album. Creative painting techniques and an egg-carton-pulp plaque contribute to the cover's lavish look.

You'll also need:

- two plastic buckets
- rubber gloves
- blender
- paper towels
- wood glue
- cheesecloth
- tan acrylic paint
- paintbrushes
- craft glue
- bronze, copper, and antique copper metallic acrylic paint
- natural sponge pieces
- gold leaf and adhesive
- antiquing glaze
- gold metallic paint pen

pretty
pocket journal

1. Center the short edges of the cardboard pieces $1/4$" apart on the wrong side of the large gift wrap piece; glue in place. Glue the paper over the edges of the cardboard pieces.

2. Glue dark green ribbon around the center of the cover, then glue gold ribbon along the edge of the dark green ribbon. Glue a V of gold ribbon, then a button to the front cover.

3. For the ties, glue the ends of the green ribbon pieces inside the cover edges.

4. Stack the paper strips together; fold in half, then unfold. Stitch the pages together along the fold.

5. Glue the bottom page to the inside back cover. Glue the small piece of gift wrap to the inside front cover.

Snippets of ribbon and gift wrap adorn this itty-bitty book. Small enough to stash in a pocket or purse, our tiny journal could hold anything from diary entries to your grocery list.

Recycled items:
- two 3" x $4^3/4$" pieces of heavy-weight cardboard
- 4" x $10^1/4$" piece and a $2^3/4$" x $4^1/2$" piece of heavy-weight gift wrap
- 2" wide dark green, and gold and green narrow ribbon pieces
- button
- twelve $2^3/4$" x $9^1/2$" strips of blank paper

You'll also need:
- craft glue

creative
place card

Whether you're hosting a large bash or an intimate get-together, our winsome place cards are sure to strike a pleasant chord with your guests. Choose scraps of tissue paper and embellishments to coordinate with your party theme.

1. Cut a 6" x 7" piece from card stock. Matching short edges, score card and fold it in half.

2. Stamp and emboss images onto several coordinating pieces of tissue paper. Tear tissue into pieces, then overlapping the pieces, *Découpage* them onto the front of the card.

3. Glue embellishing items to front of card.

4. For tag, cut a 2" x 3$\frac{1}{2}$" rectangle from folder; cut diagonally across corners at one end of rectangle. Draw around it on folder, then cut out $\frac{1}{8}$" inside drawn lines.

5. Write name on center of small tag. *Découpage* tissue paper over tag, then small pieces around edges for a border. Draw over name with paint pen. Glue small tag to center of large tag, then punch a hole through tag. Fold several lengths of thread in half, then thread the loop through the hole; insert the ends through the loop, then pull the thread taut. Glue a bead above the hole.

Crafting Techniques:
• *Découpage*, page 157

Recycled items:
• decorative tissue paper
• embellishing items (we used beads, lace, and metallic

You'll also need:
• heavy-weight card stock
• rubber stamp and ink pad
• embossing powder and heat gun
• antique découpage finish
• craft glue
• paint pen
• hole punch

charming postcard set

Hi Erin!
I hope you
are enjoying
your new home
and new friends.
I'll see you in a
few weeks!
I can't wait !!
Love,
Aunt Becky

To: Erin Sutter
5270 Cypress Creek
Spring, TX
73 0

Send your love long distance with our graceful stamped postcard collection. The cards and holder are made from manila file folders, while the heartwarming stamp is cut from a surprising source — a computer mouse pad!

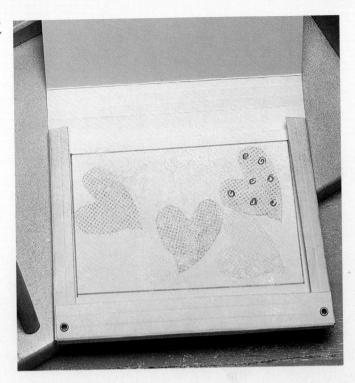

Recycled items:
- manila folders
- foam mouse pad
- corrugated cardboard
- small lid for stamping circles

You'll also need:
- craft knife and cutting pad
- eyelets and eyelet tool kit
- craft glue
- gold and assorted colors of ink pads
- permanent markers

Allow glue and ink to dry after each application.

1. Referring to the postcard ensemble diagram on page 148, draw the card holder on the inside of one of the folders. Cut out the holder; lightly score, then fold along the dotted lines. Cut out 4" x 6" postcards from folders.

2. Follow manufacturer's instructions to attach eyelets to the bottom flap. Leaving ¹/₄" along the top edge unglued, glue the bottom flap to the side flaps.

3. Use the gold ink pad to lightly stamp the card holder and postcards.

4. To make heart stamp, cut a heart shape from the mouse pad and cardboard; glue the smooth side of the mouse pad heart to the cardboard heart. Stamp hearts and circles and draw swirls and dots on the holder cover and the postcards; draw a border along the front edges.

5. Place the postcards in the holder and fold the cover down matchbook-style.

> *Tip:*
> *For standard postal postcard rate, a postcard can be 3¹/₂" x 5" minimum to 4¹/₄" x 6" maximum in size.*

framed friendship collage

Allow paint, glue, and sealer to dry after each application.

1. Working on flat side of the frame and mitering strips at the corners, cut strips of lightbulb packaging to fit the frame. Paint the frame black and the strips copper. Using a stencil brush, dab red and black paint on the strips. Glue the strips to the frame.

2. For background, cut a piece of cardboard to fit in the frame. Paint the background light yellow. Arrange the book pages on the background as desired and glue in place. Spray with sealer.

3. Wipe the pages with a watery mixture of yellow paint. Lightly *Dry Brush* background with copper, red, and yellow paint, then lightly *Spatter Paint* with black paint.

4. Mitering at corners, cut 1/4" wide strips of cardboard to fit along edges of background; paint strips black and glue in place. Glue background into back of frame.

Crafting Techniques:
- *Dry Brush*, page 158
- *Spatter Paint*, page 158

5. Cut two hearts from cardboard. Trim around one heart with craft scissors. Paint the large heart black and the small heart red; spray red heart with sealer. Dab red heart with a paper towel dipped in watery yellow paint mixture. Glue red heart to black heart, then glue picture to red heart. Attach heart to background using foam spacers.

Recycled items:
- frame
- lightbulb packaging
- heavy-weight cardboard (we used legal pad backing)
- pages from a book (you could photocopy them if desired)
- photograph

You'll also need:
- black, copper, red, light yellow, and yellow acrylic paint
- paintbrushes
- stencil brush
- craft glue
- matte clear acrylic spray sealer
- toothbrush
- decorative-edge craft scissors
- self-adhesive foam spacers

Lifelong friends are few and far between. Honor one of these kindred spirits with an endearing tribute crafted from a timeworn picture frame. Pages torn from an old book provide an interesting backdrop for the cherished photo.

hobby
display

Trains, planes, or automobiles — whatever your passion, this hobby shelf is a sharp way to show it off. Appropriate "tiles" are cut from old magazines or calendars and attached to a shallow wooden tray. How simple!

Our drawer measures 11" x 17½", we cut our pictures into 1" squares, and we left ¼" between each picture piece.

1. Remove any dividers from tray. Prime, then paint tray black.

2. Cut a piece of cardboard to fit inside tray.

3. Position pictures on cardboard to determine size and spacing. Apply double-sided adhesive to backs of pictures. Trim pictures to an equal size.

4. Cut pictures into six equal pieces. Spacing evenly, remove backing and smooth pictures onto cardboard.

5. Apply double-sided adhesive to card stock. Cut strips of card stock slightly wider than the spaces between the pictures. Cut border strips to cover outer edges. Remove backing, then smooth the strips and border into place.

6. Use spray adhesive to secure the card stock in the tray.

Recycled items:
- wooden tray or drawer
- cardboard
- pictures cut from magazines

You'll also need:
- spray primer
- black spray paint
- rotary cutter and cutting mat
- black card stock
- double-sided self adhesive sheets
- spray adhesive

Tip:
For really straight lines, use a rotary cutter and cutting mat to cut pictures apart!

whimsical paper collage

A creative medium for any budding artist, handmade paper is easy to infuse with colors and textures. Scraps of fabric give this collage an abstract, imaginative look — sans paint!

1. Follow the steps for *Getting Ready* and *Making the Paper* to make a thick sheet of paper.

2. Place bits and pieces of fabric and ribbon on the paper. To dry the paper, place another piece of muslin on top of the stack, then place the stack on a flat surface between several towels.

3. Place a flat board, then a heavy book on top and allow the paper to dry for several days. Carefully remove the fabrics and ribbons from the paper to reveal the textures and colors that have been left behind. Remove the paper from the muslin and allow to dry completely on a flat surface.

Recycled items:
- handmade paper
- fabric and ribbon scraps

You'll also need:
- muslin
- thin flat board
- towels
- heavy book

Crafting Techniques:
- *Getting Ready*, page 52
- *Making the Paper*, page 52

making
handmade paper

*For **paper clay**, follow Step 1 of Making the Paper to prepare pulp mixture. Drain pulp and add 6 tablespoons of wood glue per cup of pulp.*

Getting Ready

1. Prepare the screen. Place the frame flat side down on screen. Pulling screen taut, staple screen to the molded side of the frame. Trim the screen even with the inner edges of the frame.

2. Prepare a surface to remove the paper from the screen. Place several towels on a flat surface, then cover the towels with muslin.

Making the Paper

1. Tear paper into small pieces – about 1" square. Place the paper pieces in a bowl and soak in warm water for about an hour. Place 5 cups of water and a golf ball-size ball of soaked paper in blender. Blend the mixture on high for ten seconds, three or four times.

2. Pour pulp into the tub. Repeat Step 1 to fill tub to 2" from the top. If desired, add threads or dried flower pieces to the tub. Add one cup liquid starch, then stir the mixture.

3. Holding the screen, frame side down, lower the screen into the tub down one side. Slowly pull the screen straight up out of the mixture.

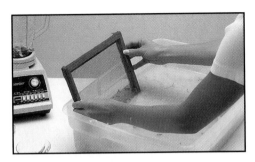

2. Peel off the top muslin piece, then lift one corner of the paper and peel it off the bottom piece.

4. To remove the paper from the screen, carefully place one edge of the screen on the prepared surface. Lower the screen onto the muslin, then blot the screen to remove excess water. Carefully remove screen.

Recycled items:
- wooden frame (we used a 16" x 20" frame)
- piece of fine screen larger than opening in frame
- uncoated paper pieces (pullout advertisement cards from magazines work great)
- pieces of thread (optional)

You'll also need:
- staple gun
- towels
- large bowls
- blender
- large rectangular tub (big enough for the frame to fit in easily)
- liquid starch
- bleached muslin pieces (at least 2" larger on all sides than the frame)

Drying the Paper
1. Place the muslin and paper on an ironing surface. Place a second piece of muslin on top of the paper. Using a dry iron set on cotton, iron the stack on both sides until the paper is dry.

showcase
box

A cardboard candy box is the basis for this sweet keepsake container. Embellished with handmade paper and bits of ribbon and jewelry, it's just the place to store sentimental letters and mementos.

Recycled items:
- breath mint tin with lid removed
- candy box with lid
- net produce bag
- handmade paper (see page 52)
- piece torn from page of book
- charm
- ribbon bow
- lightbulb packaging
- corrugated cardboard with paper removed from both sides

You'll also need:
- craft glue
- desired color of paint for box
- paintbrushes
- desired color of spray fabric paint to tint handmade paper and coordinating ink pad
- green and gold ink pads
- copper craft wire
- hot glue gun

Use craft glue for all gluing unless otherwise indicated.

1. Draw around tin at center of lid; cut out opening just inside drawn lines. Glue a piece of netting over opening, then paint box.

2. Tear pieces of handmade paper slightly smaller than sides and top of box; tear hole in center of top piece slightly smaller than opening. Spritz paper pieces with fabric paint, then stamp the edges with the coordinating ink pad. Glue pieces to box.

3. Line bottom of tin with a piece of handmade paper; glue paper in to secure. Arrange and glue piece from book, charm, ribbon bow, and a coiled wire shape in box. Hot glue tin to inside of lid under opening.

4. For each arrow on top of box, cut a 1/2" x 2" piece from lightbulb packaging. Cut one end to a point and other end in a V; stamp ridges with green ink pad. Tear a small piece from corrugated cardboard; stamp ridges with the gold ink pad. Thread a length of wire up through the holes of a button, twist together to tighten, then curl the ends around a paintbrush handle.

5. Glue an arrow, cardboard piece, then wired button at each corner on top of box.

handcrafted
card

Create this exquisite greeting card in a twinkling with handmade paper, rubber stamps, and some surprising materials. Delicate shading is achieved with decorative chalks, while the star's tail is made from a frayed backpack strap!

1. Dampen a piece of handmade paper, large enough to cover the star stamp, on both sides. Press the paper over the stamp to mold the paper; carefully tear the edges of the paper around the edges of the star. Set aside to dry.

2. While the molded paper is drying, fold the card stock in half. Use craft scissors to cut a piece of decorative paper slightly smaller than the front of the card. Stamp the paper with the gold ink pad. Following the manufacturer's instructions, use eyelets to attach the paper to the front of the card.

3. Tear a piece of handmade paper slightly smaller than the decorative paper. Spritz paper piece with paint, then stamp the edges of the paper with the coordinating ink pad. Glue the paper to the card.

4. Glue a 1" wide piece of gauze fabric down the left side of the card. Unravel a length of string from the strap piece; wrap it several times around the card front over the gauze strip. Thread the pendant onto the string and tie the string into a bow.

5. Lightly color the star with desired colors of chalk, then stamp the center with a gold swirl design. Carefully remove the paper star from the stamp. Glue the strap piece to the back of the star, then glue the star to the card.

Recycled items:
- handmade paper (see page 52)
- gauze fabric
- piece of nylon strap
- pendant or charm

You'll also need:
- star-shaped rubber stamp
- 8½" x 11" piece of card stock
- decorative-edge craft scissors
- decorative paper
- gold ink pad
- eyelets and eyelet tool kit
- desired color of spray fabric paint to tint handmade paper and coordinating color ink pad
- craft glue
- colored chalk
- swirl design rubber stamp

Tip:
Speed up the drying time of your molded paper by using a hair dryer to dry the paper.

graceful
gift tag

Like icing on a birthday cake, an enchanting tag adds a little something extra to even the prettiest present. Create this thoughtful keepsake with a manila folder, handmade paper, and crafty scraps.

1. Cut a 2¹/₂" x 4¹/₄" rectangle from folder; cut diagonally across corners at one end of rectangle. Tear a piece of handmade paper ¹/₄" smaller than folder piece. Spritz both pieces with paint; glue paper piece to folder piece.

2. Following the manufacturer's instructions, use an eyelet to attach the pieces together.

3. Wrap wire around a paintbrush handle to make two wire curls. Tear a 1" x 2" piece from handmade paper; write desired greeting on paper piece. Glue the wire curls, a 1¹/₂" square of corrugated cardboard, a square of gauze fabric, then the greeting on the tag.

4. Glue a charm to the tag and add a gauze hanger through the eyelet.

Recycled items:
- manila folder
- handmade paper (see page 52)
- corrugated cardboard with paper removed from one side
- gauze fabric scraps
- charm

You'll also need:
- desired color of spray fabric paint to tint handmade paper
- craft glue
- eyelet and eyelet tool kit
- gold craft wire

pleated-paper
greeting card

Send your best wishes via this unique greeting card. The colorful paper shapes, folded accordion-style, make an original statement for any occasion.

Recycled items:
- decorative paper pieces and gift bags
- decorative yarn

You'll also need:
- 8 1/2" x 11" piece of card stock
- craft glue
- tracing paper
- black permanent pen

1. Fold the piece of card stock in half. Glue a piece of decorative paper to the front of the card.

2. Cut one 3/4" x 11" strip and two 1/2" x 11" strips from the gift bag. For each flower, fold one strip accordion-style; glue the ends together to form a circle. Glue the flowers to the card.

3. Trace the butterfly pattern, page 155, onto tracing paper; cut out. Use the pattern to cut a butterfly from the gift bag. Fold the butterfly accordion-style, then glue it to the card.

4. Draw a butterfly trail, then write a message on the card.

5. Tie decorative yarn around the fold of the card.

Tip:
If the paper you want to use for the flower isn't long enough, overlap and glue the ends of two strips together!

lovely little
gift box

Découpaged with a floral napkin, our custom-made gift box is a wonderful way to present a tiny treat. Embellish your personal version with animal designs, words, or whatever strikes your fancy. The possibilities are endless!

1. Sizing as desired, use the box pattern on page 149 to cut a box from the folder.

2. Unfold and press the napkins; separate into layers. Apply spray adhesive to the right side of the box, then smooth the printed napkin layer onto the box; trim the napkin even with the box edges.

3. Fold, then glue the box together with the flaps to the inside.

4. Apply a coat of glue to the box. Trim around the designs on the front edge of the box.

Recycled item:
• manila folder

You'll also need:
• decorative napkins with all-over designs
• spray adhesive
• craft glue

Tip:
Position the napkin along the front edge, so when trimmed, it will create a pretty border.

mosaic kitchen caddy

Keep your cooking utensils close by with a clever kitchen caddy. Cheerful paper "tiles" transform a cardboard snack canister into this handy (and handsome) organizer.

1. Paint canister white; allow to dry. Cover the inside with paper.

2. Cut $3/8$" squares from the same color cardboard; leaving a small space between all pieces, glue the squares to the canister in blocks of nine.

3. Cut random shapes from another color cardboard. Leaving a small space between all pieces, glue shapes to canister to fill in remaining surface of canister.

Recycled items:
- cardboard snack canister
- cereal boxes

You'll also need:
- white spray paint
- self-adhesive paper
- craft glue

Tip:
Use marbles to weight the canister.

61

newborn announcements

It's a Girl Announcement

1. Cut a 4^3/$_4$" x 7^3/$_4$" piece of decorative paper for the background. Glue ribbon-threaded pieces of computer paper along the edges of the background, then glue buttons down center.

2. For flower, use craft scissors to cut a 2^1/$_2$" dia. circle from white paper; cut out a 2" dia. circle from center of flower. Cut out pieces of cereal bag and coordinating paper to fit behind opening; write phrase on paper piece. Layer and glue coordinating paper, cereal bag piece, then flower on background. Zigzag stitch around opening.

3. For pocket, cut a 3^1/$_4$" x 4" piece from cereal bag. Sew pocket to right-hand side of background.

4. For tag, cut a 2^3/$_4$" x 4^3/$_4$" rectangle from gift box; cut diagonally across corners at one end of the rectangle. Cut a piece of decorative paper slightly smaller than the tag. Glue paper to tag. Write birth information on tag. Punch a hole though top of tag, then loop a piece of string though the hole.

5. Use craft scissors to cut out a 5^1/$_2$" x 8^1/$_2$" piece of cardboard; glue background to cardboard piece. Place tag in pocket.

It's a Boy Announcement

1. Cut two 3^3/$_4$" x 4^3/$_4$" pieces of coordinating papers for backgrounds.

2. For pocket, cut a 3^1/$_4$" x 4" piece from cereal bag. Sew pocket to one background piece.

3. For tag, cut a 2^3/$_4$" x 4^3/$_4$" rectangle from gift box; cut diagonally across corners at one end of the rectangle. Cut a piece of decorative paper slightly smaller than the tag. Glue paper to tag. Write birth information on tag. Punch a hole though top of tag, then loop a piece of string though the hole.

4. For rattle, cut a 2" dia. circle in remaining background piece. Cut a piece of coordinating paper and cereal bag to fit behind circle. Write phrase on coordinating paper. Place paper dots on paper piece. Glue cereal bag piece to paper piece along edges, then glue piece behind opening in background. Sew along the edge of the opening.

5. For handle, glue a length of computer paper strip onto decorative paper. Use craft scissors to trim the edges, then glue handle to the background.

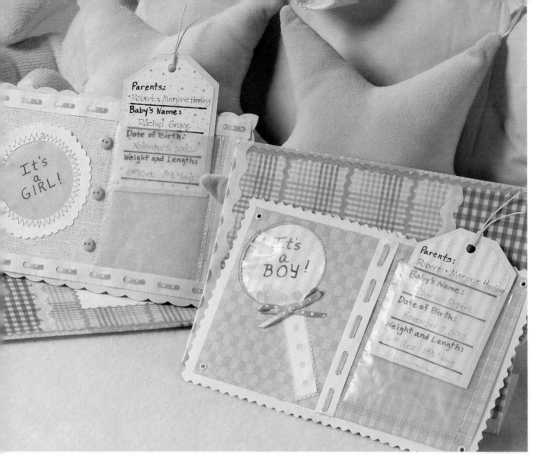

Proclaim the joyful news of your recent arrival with handcrafted birth announcements. Lightweight cardboard and gift wrap make these charming cards as unique as your own special delivery.

6. Use craft scissors to cut a 5¹/₂" x 8¹/₂" piece of cardboard; glue backgrounds to cardboard piece. Trim card with a ribbon-threaded computer paper strip, eyelets, and a bow. Place tag in pocket.

Envelope

1. Cut a 9³/₄" x 14" piece from wrapping paper. Fold and glue long edges ¹/₂" to wrong side. Fold one end 6" to wrong side. Glue edges together to form envelope.

2. Insert announcement, then fold and glue flap down to close.

Recycled items:
- decorative paper
- ribbon and buttons
- form feed strips from computer paper
- white pieces of paper
- wax paper liner from cereal box
- decorative gift box
- string
- lightweight cardboard
- paper dots punched from hole punch

You'll also need:
- craft glue
- decorative-edge craft scissors
- 2" dia. hole punch
- eyelets and an eyelet tool kit
- wrapping paper

playful
paper bouquet

Add a splash of color to any room in your home with a basket of brilliant handmade flowers. Fashioned from recycled greeting cards, the bouquet can be bold and sassy or subtly elegant, depending on the shades you select.

Tip:
Extra leaves can be attached to short stem pieces to fill basket.

1. Trace the petal pattern on page 148 onto tracing paper; cut out. For each flower, use pattern to cut eleven petals from one color of cards.

2. Prime, then paint acorn to coordinate with petals. Glue bristles around acorn. Fill cap with hot glue, then attach acorn.

3. Glue five petals around cap. Wrap a rubber band around cap to help hold petals in place. Repeat to glue remaining petals around cap.

4. For each stem, straighten two hangers; remove hook ends. Wrap hangers together with masking tape. Hot glue stem to bottle cap. Wrap bottle cap and stem with floral tape. Trim stem to desired height.

5. Trace the leaf pattern on page 148 onto tracing paper; cut out. Draw around pattern on various green cards for the number of leaves desired. Attach leaves to stem with floral tape.

6. Paint basket as desired. Use hot glue to secure floral foam in basket. Cover foam with moss, then arrange flowers in basket.

snowman
gift bag

This frosty gift tote is a wintry way to dress up a special holiday present. Use shredded paper and glue to sculpt the delightfully textured snow friend.

Allow glue to dry after each application unless otherwise indicated.

1. Cut a cardboard box to the desired height to fit your gift. Prime, then paint the box blue. Draw a snowman scene on the box.

2. Mix several handfuls of crumpled shredded paper with glue until completely saturated. Shape a small nose out of the paper mixture and set it aside to dry. Fill in the scene with the mixture.

3. Paint the nose orange and the scene white. Using a mixture of one part blue and three parts white paint, add *Shading* to the scene as desired. Add white paint to the scene where glitter is desired, and use the end of the brush to make white "snowflakes" on the box; apply glitter to the wet paint.

4. Glue the nose, eyes, and remaining buttons in place. Draw several dots for the mouth.

5. For the scarf, cut two strips of fleece; fringe one end of each strip and slightly curve the opposite ends. Glue the scarf in place.

6. Glue trim around the top of the box.

7. For each handle, punch two holes through the top of the box. Thread a length of cord through the holes and knot each end on the inside of the box.

Recycled items:
- cardboard box (we used a 16-oz. cracker box)
- paper from a shredder
- two buttons for eyes and three small buttons
- fleece, decorative trim, and cord pieces

You'll also need:
- acrylic primer
- blue, orange, and white acrylic paint
- paintbrushes
- craft glue
- iridescent glitter
- black permanent marker
- hole punch

Crafting Technique:
- *Shading*, page 158

christmas
memory page

Christmas is caring...

SURPRISES

...and sharing.

HUGS

happy memories

Enjoy the special moments this season brings.

Christmas is a time of giving

Smiles

HAPPY CHRISTMAS

Trimmed in shades of red and green, our memory page will be a very merry addition to your scrapbook. Fashioned from holiday-theme tissue paper and an assortment of favorite cards, this jolly collage is full of scrappy spirit.

1. Measure the scrapbook page; cut a piece from tissue paper the determined measurements, then glue it to the page.

2. Cut frames from the cards. Frame your favorite photos.

3. Use craft scissors to cut out words, phrases, and motifs from cards.

4. Arrange and glue the photos and phrases on the page. Apply eyelets to some of the frames, if desired.

Recycled items:
- Christmas-motif tissue paper
- greeting cards
- photographs

You'll also need:
- scrapbook page
- spray adhesive
- decorative-edge craft scissors
- eyelets and an eyelet tool kit (optional)

> *Tip:*
> To ensure safety and a long life for your photos, apply an acid-free spray to items (and allow to dry)

attic

caches

and

flea

market

finds

hidden
treasures

It's surprisingly simple to create clever
furnishings and accessories from attic
caches and flea market finds! Transform
a wooden bench into a novel reading
table. Use cork coasters and more to
turn a metal tin into a memo
canister. Brighten a patchwork
throw with tablecloth blocks, or dress
up a treasure box with bits of jewelry.
How lovely!

nostalgic
bedroom set

Springtime is in the air when you dress up your bedroom with this dreamy ensemble. Silk flower petals embellish the bedside table, and the queen-size headboard is fashioned from a wooden crib.

Allow glue and paint to dry after each application unless otherwise indicated.

1. Place crib pieces, right-side down and side by side, on a flat surface, then wood glue the pieces together for a headboard. Use mending braces along the center back to secure pieces together. Turn the headboard right-side up. Cut a piece of molding to cover the crack down the center, then glue it in place.

2. Prime the headboard and table; mask areas on the table to be painted purple. Paint the headboard and table black. Apply a thin layer of wax along some of the edges and raised areas on the headboard and table; paint the headboard and table green. Lightly sand the waxed areas for an aged look, then wipe with the tack cloth. Remove tape and paint masked areas purple.

3. Cut pieces of decorative paper to fit on the headboard as desired; *Découpage* the pieces in place.

4. Remove the plastic centers from the flowers. Punch holes in the fabric scrap; glue one fabric dot to the center of each flower, then glue the flowers to the tabletop. Follow manufacturer's instructions to laminate the tabletop.

Crafting Technique
• *Découpage*, page 157

Tip:
If your crib doesn't have an area to découpage, you can attach a piece of hardboard to the frame and decorate it.

Recycled items:
• identical head and footboards from a wooden crib
• remnant of flat molding
• small wooden table
• decorative tissue paper
• silk flowers (we used hydrangeas)
• scrap of pink fabric

You'll also need:
• wood glue
• mending braces
• spray primer
• painter's masking tape
• black and green spray paint
• paste floor wax
• sandpaper
• tack cloth
• purple acrylic paint
• paintbrushes
• découpage glue
• hole punch
• laminating top coat

beribboned
memo basket

Turn a flat-bottomed basket into an inventive place to display photos, notes, and more. Bold buttons and ribbons provide a cheerful contrast to the plaid placemat background.

1. Apply primer, then paint to the basket.

2. Cover the front of the cardboard with batting and fabric. Gluing the ends to the back, use lengths of ribbon to shape evenly spaced diamonds on the front of the covered piece. Working through all layers, sew buttons through some of the ribbon intersections.

3. For a hanger, loop a length of wire through each top back corner of the basket and twist ends together. Glue the covered piece in the basket.

Recycled items:
- wicker basket (we used a 7³/₄" x 14" x 3¹/₂" basket)
- corrugated cardboard to fit in basket
- polyester batting remnant
- dish towel, large fabric placemat, or fabric remnant
- ribbons
- buttons
- craft wire

You'll also need:
- spray primer
- spray paint
- hot glue gun
- heavy-duty needle and thread

petite tray table

An ingenious addition to a sunroom or porch, this dainty table keeps a cool drink or a magazine within reach. Construct your own using a plant stand, an embossed aluminum platter, and an array of metal paints.

1. Spray paint the tray and stand. Use metal paint to paint the embossed designs on the tray. Apply two coats of sealer to the top of the tray.

2. Follow the welding compound manufacturer's instructions to attach the tray to the stand.

Recycled items:
- large embossed metal serving tray
- metal plant stand or table legs

You'll also need:
- spray paint for tray and stand
- metal paints
- paintbrushes
- clear acrylic spray sealer
- welding compound

Tip:
If your tray doesn't have an embossed design, you can transfer, then paint a design on it...or just freehand your own design!

blooming
arrangement

Brimming with blossoms, an old-timey suitcase is a welcome addition to the entryway or living room. Create this travel arrangement with secondhand florals and a length of favorite fabric.

1. Cut a piece of cardboard to fit inside the lid of the suitcase. Cover the cardboard piece with fabric, then spot glue the covered piece into the lid.

2. Trimming pieces as necessary to fit, tightly fill the bottom of the suitcase with packing blocks. Using floral pins to secure in place, cover the foam with sheet moss, then insert the stems of the floral pieces and greenery into the foam.

3. Place the figurine in the arrangement. Drape a piece of fabric over the lid and around the arrangement.

Recycled items:
- corrugated cardboard
- hard-backed suitcase
- fabric remnant
- plastic foam packing blocks
- dried or silk floral and greenery pieces
- figurine

You'll also need:
- hot glue gun
- floral pins
- dried sheet moss

Tip:
If the suitcase has that not-so-fresh smell, place a few briquettes of charcoal in it and close the lid for a few days...the smell should be gone!

handy
cook's desk

Whether jotting down an ingredient substitution or leisurely reading a new cookbook, this cast-off desk is a pretty place to pore over your recipe collection. A ruffled slipcover and painted plaid pattern add a delicate air.

Use a ½" seam allowance for all sewing unless otherwise indicated.

1. Apply primer to desk; spray metal parts of desk white. Paint back slats and table as desired...we painted our table green, then *Dry Brushed* it with white paint. Apply two coats of sealer to desk.

2. Draw around seat on newsprint, then cut out for a pattern. Use pattern to cut a cushion from foam. Draw around pattern on wrong side of one fabric; cut out cover 2" outside drawn lines.

3. Place cover on seat and mark back corners of cover where back attaches to seat; mark equal spaces on the front "corners" of the cover. For each set of ruffles, measure between the marks on one side of the cover and double that measurement; cut one 7" wide and one 13" wide strip by the determined measurement from coordinating fabrics. Matching right sides, fold each strip in half lengthwise and sew the ends together; clip the corners and turn right-side out. Matching raw edges, stack the narrow strip on the wide strip; baste together along raw edges. Gather ruffles to fit between marks on cover; matching raw edges, pin to right side of cover, then sew in place. Repeat for each side of cover.

4. Make a small pleat in front corners, then sew buttons over pleats to secure.

5. For each chair tie, cut a 2" x 20" strip from fabric. Matching right sides, fold strip in half lengthwise and sew the long edges together; trim seam allowance and clip corners, then turn tie right-side out. Cut tie in half; sew one end of each strip to the underside of each mark at the back corners.

6. Place cushion on chair and cover over cushion; tie chair ties to chair.

Recycled items:
- school desk
- newsprint
- coordinating fabric remnants

You'll also need:
- white acrylic spray primer
- white spray paint
- acrylic paint
- paintbrushes
- clear acrylic spray sealer
- 1"-thick foam

Crafting Technique
- *Dry Brush*, page 158

stack-art
candlesticks

Eclectic candlesticks give a simple side table an artistic aura. Dress up wooden blocks, bowls, and more with a variety of painting techniques for individual appeal.

1. For each candlestick, arrange and glue wooden items together. Apply primer and desired base coat to candlestick.

2. Paint designs on the candlestick. For the "sponge-crackled" look, mix a few drops of blending medium with a small amount of paint. Crumple a piece of cheesecloth and dip it into the mixture; lightly blot the cheesecloth on a foam plate, then dab color onto the candlestick. Repeat until the desired effect is achieved.

3. Apply two coats of sealer to the candlestick.

Recycled items:
- assorted wooden items: bowls, napkin rings, candle cups, children's blocks, and salt and pepper shakers

You'll also need:
- wood glue
- spray primer
- assorted acrylic paints
- paintbrushes
- blending medium
- cheesecloth
- clear acrylic spray sealer

tiny
treasure box

Embossing powder gives this cast-off jewelry box a brilliant shimmer, while bits of jewelry create a fancy flourish. Fill with tiny tokens or use as a gift box for an elegant present. Splendid!

1. Paint box black. Working in small sections, stamp ink pad on lid, then immediately sprinkle inked area with embossing powder; heat until powder is melted. Layering as necessary for desired thickness, repeat process while embossed areas are still soft and hot. Emboss entire lid.

2. Arrange and glue jewelry items and the eyepiece (glue decorative paper to the concave side of the lens) on the box lid.

Recycled items:
- small box with lid
- jewelry pieces and an eyepiece
- scrap of decorative paper

You'll also need:
- black acrylic paint
- paintbrush
- copper pigment ink pad
- verdigris embossing powder
- craft heat gun
- clear-drying household adhesive

> *Tip:*
> *Before the last layer of embossing powder sets, jewelry items can be pressed into the pliable surface…allow to harden around jewelry before gluing remaining items on.*

vintage patchwork throw

Use a 1/2" seam allowance for all sewing and match right sides and raw edges unless otherwise indicated. Refer to the Quilt Diagram, page 152, for cutting out pieces and assembling the quilt top.

1. For the quilt top, refer to the diagram to cut pieces from tablecloths, curtains, or fabric remnants. Cut 61" x 73" pieces from the bedspread (quilt back) and batting.

2. For the quilt center, sew three squares together to form a row; make four rows. Sew the four rows together to form a rectangle. Working on the right side of the fabric, baste the braid flange along the quilt center raw edges.

3. For the side borders, sew one 5" x 49" strip, then one 9" x 49" strip to each side of the quilt center. For the top border, sew one 5" x 37" strip and one 9" x 37" strip together; sew one square to each end. Repeat for the bottom border. Sew borders to the quilt center.

4. Working on the right side of the fabric, baste one edge of the rickrack 1/4" from the raw edges of the quilt top.

5. Place quilt top and back together, then place on batting. Working from the center outward, smooth out any wrinkles and use safety pins to pin layers together about every 12"; use straight pins to pin edges of layers together. Leaving an opening for turning, sew all edges together; remove pins. Turn the quilt right-side out, then sew the opening closed.

6. Working through all layers, use floss to sew a button to the corners of each square in the quilt center.

Recycled items:
- fabric tablecloths, curtains, or fabric remnants
- chenille bedspread
- buttons

You'll also need:
- polyester batting
- 1" wide loop braid
- jumbo rickrack
- embroidery floss

Nothing is quite so inviting as an old-fashioned patchwork throw. Backed with chenille, blocks cut from vintage tablecloths encourage a trip down memory lane, while buttons and trims add a playful touch.

practical shadow box

1. Referring to Fig. 1, cut the top from the storage box.

Fig. 1

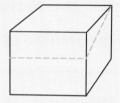

2. Overlapping at back of storage box, glue a piece of beach mat around the box; trim mat even with top of box. Glue jute along top and bottom edges of the box.

3. Paint the inside of the small box. Cut a piece of foam to cover the inside bottom of the box and glue it in place. Arrange and glue display items on the foam.

4. For the lid, remove the back from the picture frame and secure glass in frame. Center and glue small box to back of frame. Place lid on storage box.

> *Tip:*
> *If the frame does not rest centered on the storage box, stack and glue several strips of cardboard together under the front edge of the frame.*

Recycled items:
- sturdy cardboard box for storage
- straw beach mat
- jute
- cardboard box that will fit in storage box, but is smaller than picture frame and larger than glass
- sheet packing foam
- items to display
- wooden picture frame (with glass) slightly larger than storage box
- corrugated cardboard (optional)

You'll also need:
- hot glue gun
- acrylic paint
- paintbrushes

Covered with a straw mat and topped off with a picture-frame lid, this brag box is the epitome of stylish storage. Fill with photos or other hobby memorabilia, and you'll really have something to boast about!

scrap-happy
pillow

Raid your scrap basket for materials to make this dainty round pillow. Use buttons, doilies, and bits of fabric that have personal meaning — your family will cherish this unique keepsake.

Use a ½" seam allowance for all sewing unless otherwise indicated.

1. Adding 1" for the seam allowance, cut two circles the desired size for a pillow from fabric. Measure around one circle, then double the measurement and add 1"; cut a 6" wide by the determined measurement ruffle from fabric. Matching right sides, sew ends of ruffle together. Matching wrong sides, fold ruffle in half lengthwise and baste raw edges together.

Matching raw edges and gathering ruffle to fit, baste ruffle to right side of one pillow piece.

2. Stack and glue doilies together. Determine size for yo-yo; cut a circle of batting the determined size and a circle of fabric twice the determined size. Baste along fabric edges; center batting on wrong side of fabric, gather fabric over batting, and knot threads to secure. Sew a button to center of yo-yo, then glue it to the doilies. Sew buttons to attach doilies to the right side of remaining pillow piece.

3. Matching right sides and raw edges and leaving an opening for turning, sew pillow pieces together. Turn right-side out, stuff pillow, then sew opening closed.

Recycled items:
- coordinating fabric remnants
- two round fabric doilies
- batting scrap
- buttons

You'll also need:
- fabric glue
- polyester fiberfill

engaging
server

Elegance meets individuality in these polished serving stands. Fill the bowl of the inverted goblet with various notions for the perfect complement to a bridal shower or other fancy party.

Arrange the dishes so the pieces fit together; disassemble. Arrange the decorative items inside the goblet, or glue them to the center bottom of one saucer or bowl…invert the goblet onto the saucer, covering the decorative items, then glue it in place. Stack and glue the remaining dishes together.

Recycled items:
- clear glass dishes and goblet
- decorative items to fit inside goblet

You'll also need:
- clear-drying silicone adhesive

reading table

Use household adhesive for all gluing unless otherwise indicated.

1. Prime, then paint the bench and frame brown. *Dry Brush* the painted pieces gold. Paint the accent pieces and the edges of each book's pages gold.

2. For each book, use craft glue to adhere the front and back covers to the first and last pages of the book. Cover the page edges with a layer of craft glue.

3. Choose two of the books to be glued upright. Arrange several books into a stack the same height as the upright books. Glue the stack of books together, then to the center of the bench. Glue the upright books to the bench at each end of the stack.

4. For the tabletop, overlapping and covering the front of the hardboard piece, use the glue stick to adhere pages from a book to the hardboard piece; trim the pages even with the sides of the board. Secure the glass and board in the frame.

5. Glue the tabletop to the books.

Recycled items:
- wooden bench
- wooden picture frame with glass
- hardbound books all near the same size
- piece of hardboard to fit in frame
- thin wooden pieces (optional)

You'll also need:
- acrylic primer
- paintbrushes
- brown and metallic gold acrylic paint
- three wooden accent pieces
- craft glue
- clear-drying household adhesive
- craft glue stick

Tip:
If your upright and stacked books are uneven, glue painted pieces of thin wood where needed to make them level.

Crafting Technique
- *Dry Brush*, page 158

Looking for a creative conversation piece? This smart little side table really stacks up. Craft your own from a small bench, an old picture frame, and several thick, hardback books.

memo canister

Our noteworthy tin can be used several ways — write messages on the painted "chalkboard," hold papers in place with washer magnets, or pin knickknacks to a coaster corkboard. Mount the canister on a "recycled" swivel plate for even more convenience, and store notions inside as needed.

1. Apply primer, then chalkboard paint to the outside of the tin and lid. Paint the rim of the lid (mask around rim with tape), the clothespin, the washers, and the printed side of the magnets silver.

2. Draw around the clothespin and washers on the magnets; cut out just inside the drawn lines. Glue the cut out magnets to the clothespin and washers.

3. Glue the swivel plate to the bottom of the tin, then glue the coaster to one side of the tin for a tack board. Stick the clothespin chalk holder and washer magnets on the tin.

Recycled items:
- metal tin with lid
- wooden clothespin
- metal washers
- advertiser's sheet magnets
- swivel plate from a lazy Susan
- cork coaster

You'll also need:
- spray primer
- black chalkboard spray paint
- painter's masking tape
- silver spray paint
- clear-drying household adhesive

Tip:
If you don't have a thick cork coaster, glue two or three thin ones together, then glue to the tin.

classic
hamper

Cleverly crafted from a folding TV tray stand and a vintage tablecloth, this blooming hamper boasts classic appeal. And clean-up couldn't be easier — just unbutton the bag and add it to the wash.

Use a ¹/₂" seam allowance for all sewing unless otherwise indicated.

1. Cut a dowel piece to fit between the top of the legs on the stand. Use screws to attach the dowel piece to the stand. Prime, then paint the stand.

2. Open the stand to the desired width, then tie a piece of string around the dowels to hold the stand's position while determining measurements.

3. Referring to Fig. 1, determine measurements for A and B; add 1" to each measurement. Cut a piece from tablecloth and one from liner fabric the determined measurements.

Fig. 1

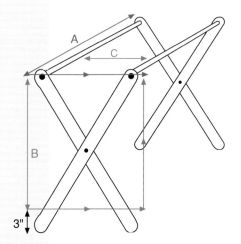

4. Matching right sides and short edges, fold the tablecloth piece in half and sew the sides together. To square the bottom, match the side seams to the bottom of the bag to form points (Fig. 2). Sew across the piece (dashed lines in Fig. 2) the measurement of C from Fig. 1. Trim seam allowance to 1/2". Turn bag right-side out.

Fig. 2

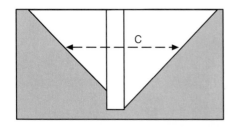

5. Leaving a 4" opening in one side seam for turning, repeat Step 4 to sew the liner together; do not turn liner right-side out.

6. Cut twelve 2" x 6" strips from the tablecloth. For each tab, match the right sides of two strips together and sew the sides and one end together; turn right-side out. Make a buttonhole in the sewn end.

7. Matching top edges of bag, with side seams of bag at center, refer to Fig. 3 to mark placements for center tabs. Matching raw edges and pinning to the right side of the fabric, pin one tab to the bag at each mark. Pin one tab around each dowel, then evenly spacing across the dowels, pin the remaining tabs to the bag and around the dowels; mark placements for buttons on bag. Remove the bag from the dowels and baste the tabs in place.

Fig. 3

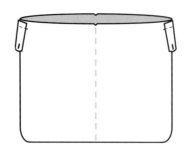

8. Matching right sides, side seams, and top edges, place the tablecloth bag inside the liner and sew the top edges together. Turn the bag right-side out through the opening in the liner, then stitch the opening closed.

9. Sew the buttons to the bag. Place the bag in the stand and button the tabs around the dowels.

Recycled items:
• wooden TV tray stand with tray removed
• piece of string
• fabric tablecloth
• large fabric remnant for liner
• six buttons

You'll also need:
• 3/4" diameter wooden dowel
• two wood screws
• spray acrylic primer
• spray paint

organized chair

Need a cool computer chair? Acrylic paint, fabric scraps, and an old spindle chair add up to the ide *solution. The best part — a variety of pockets stor* *note cards, notebooks, and everything in between.*

Allow paint to dry after each application; several coats of paint may be necessary for desired coverage. Use a ¹/₂" seam allowance for all sewing unless otherwise indicated.

1. Apply primer, then base coat to the chair. Use masking tape to outline areas to be painted with accent colors; prime the areas, then paint the desired color.

2. Refer to Fig. 1 to determine A, B, and C measurements for each panel; add 1" to each measurement. Draw a shape the determined measurements on the wrong side of fabric, then cut out the panel. Press each edge ¹/₂" to the wrong side and stitch in place.

Fig. 1

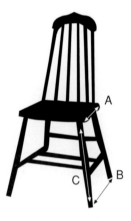

3. For each flat pocket on panel, determine the finished size for the pocket and add ¹/₂" to each measurement. For a pleated pocket, determine the finished size for the pocket and add 4¹/₂" to the width measurement. Cut out pockets the determined measurements from fabric. Press each edge ¹/₄" to the wrong side; use fusible tape to secure edges in place.

4. To pleat the pocket, press, then pin a 1" wide pleat ¹/₂" from each side at bottom of pocket (Fig. 2).

Fig. 2

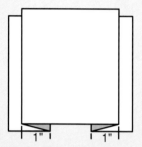

5. Use masking tape to outline the areas on the pockets to be painted. Prime, then paint the areas the desired color. Arrange the pockets on the panels and sew in place.

6. Tack the top edge of each panel to the seat.

Recycled items:
• wooden chair
• heavy-weight fabric remnants

You'll also need:
• brush-on acrylic primer
• paintbrushes
• desired base coat and accent colors of acrylic paint
• painter's masking tape
• ¹/₄" wide fusible web tape
• upholstery tacks

home
style

Enhance your home with creative accents for every room — all made with everyday castaways. Construct a trendy mirror from rolled newspaper tubes, fashion faux stone plaques from packing foam and plastic fruit, or enhance a lamp base with leather belts. Disguise a pudding cup to anchor a photo bouquet. It's oh-so-simple!

*creative accents
for every room*

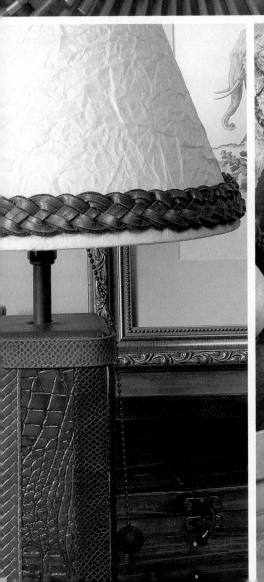

leather-clad lamp

1. Drill a hole large enough to accommodate the lamp pipe through the center of the lid and bottom of the tin.

2. Clipping corners as necessary, glue a piece of leather to the top and sides of the lid. Place the lid upside down on a cutting mat; cut an X in the leather covering the hole, then glue the leather points to the inside of the lid. Glue lid onto tin. Cut lengths from the belts to cover the sides of the tin; arrange and glue in place. Glue a belt length along the sides of the lid and the bottom edge of the tin, covering the ends of the belt lengths.

3. Remove the hardware, base, and any decorative pieces on the lamp pipe. Slide the decorated tin onto the pipe, then replace the lamp base.

4. To make a pattern of the lampshade, tape one edge of a large piece of newspaper along the seam in the lampshade. Wrap the newspaper snuggly around the shade and tape in place; cut excess paper away 1" beyond the seam in the shade. Draw along the top and bottom edges of the shade on the paper, then, leaving the paper taped to the seam on the shade, untape the outer paper and finish drawing along the shade's edges to complete the pattern. Cut excess paper away 1" outside of the drawn lines.

5. Use the pattern to cut a piece from tissue paper to cover the shade. Gently crumple the paper, then smooth it out. Apply spray adhesive to the shade, then center and smooth the paper onto the shade. Wrap the excess paper to the inside of the shade; use the glue stick to secure the paper edges in place. Glue a length of braided belt along the bottom edge of the shade. Place the shade on the lamp.

Recycled items:
- lamp with a removable base and a center pipe tall enough to accommodate tin
- tin with a lid to fit on lamp
- leather remnant
- assorted leather belts, including a braided belt
- newspaper
- lampshade to fit lamp
- large piece of tissue paper

You'll also need:
- drill and bits
- craft glue
- cutting mat and craft knife
- removable tape
- spray adhesive
- craft glue stick

Elephas maximus Linn.

Crown a distinguished desk ensemble with this handsome creation. Castoff belts make it a cinch to revive a ragtag lamp, and tissue paper gives the shade an intriguing texture.

rustic remote caddy

Distressed paint turns ordinary macaroni boxes into a country-style entertainment caddy. This charming organizer offers an attractive (and simple!) way to manage all those remote controls.

Recycled items:
- four macaroni & cheese boxes
- handle

You'll also need:
- clear-drying household adhesive
- white spray primer
- wood-tone spray
- paste floor wax
- white spray paint
- sandpaper
- tack cloth
- clear acrylic spray sealer

1. Glue two boxes together. Refer to Fig. 1 to remove the top parts from the boxes. Repeat for the remaining two boxes; glue the boxes together as shown in photo.

Fig. 1

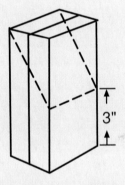

3"

2. Spray boxes with primer, then spritz with wood-tone spray. Apply wax to edges of boxes. Paint boxes white. Lightly sand waxed areas to give an aged look, then wipe with the tack cloth. Apply two coats of sealer to the boxes.

3. Glue the handle to the front of the boxes to complete the caddy.

pillared picture frame

1. For the frame, cut two pieces from the box 1" wider on each side than the desired size for frame. Draw around the photo at the center of one frame piece, then cut out window ¼" inside drawn lines. Cut two pieces from hanger tubes 2" shorter than the width of the frame; cut tubes lengthwise to slide onto frame.

2. For each column, glue caps to ends of paper towel roll; glue a length of string around roll at edge of each cap. Starting at the same point on each column, cut a slot in each roll the height of the frame.

3. Apply primer to columns, tubes, and both frame pieces. Make a glaze for each color of paint by mixing two parts glazing medium with one part paint. Working in small sections while the glaze is still wet so the colors will blend, *Sponge Paint* the pieces using the light glaze, then the medium glaze; very sparingly add the dark glaze. Use liner brush and the dark glaze to paint veins on the pieces.

4. Tape the photo behind the window, then glue the frame pieces together. Slide the sides of the frame into slots in columns, then slide and glue the tube pieces onto the top and bottom of the frame.

Crafting Technique
• *Sponge Painting*, page 158

Recycled items:
• cereal box
• photograph
• cardboard tubes from pants hangers
• four plastic beverage caps to fit on ends of rolls
• two cardboard paper towel rolls
• string

You'll also need:
• tacky glue
• spray primer
• glazing medium
• light, medium, and dark shades of desired color acrylic paint
• natural sponge
• liner paintbrush
• tape

Framed by elegant columns, this Old-World frame recalls a timeless grace.
Fashion the sturdy pillars from cardboard tubes and plastic beverage caps,
then add a sense of grandeur with delicately "marbled" paint.

net-covered
candle jar

Looking for a unique way to display a favorite candle? Take a trip down the toy aisle or through the produce section — a mesh bag does wonders for a plain glass jar! Complete the dazzling effect with ribbon and beads.

1. Slide jar into bag; place rubber band around neck of jar over mesh. Trim bag to 2" above jar.

2. Thread beads onto floss and knot ends together.

3. Catching string of beads in knot of bow, tie ribbon into a bow around neck of jar. Place the candle in the jar.

Recycled items:
- glass jar
- mesh bag to fit snugly on jar
- rubber band
- assorted beads
- embroidery floss
- wire-edged ribbon remnant

You'll also need:
- coordinating candle

"stained-glass" candle screen

A glimmer of candlelight illuminates the abstract design on our modern votive holder. Painted frames form the base of this chic candle screen, and glass paints bring the pattern to life. What a pretty picture!

1. Remove glass from frames. Apply primer, acrylic paint, and sealer to the frames.

2. Cut a piece of paper the same size as the glass to be stained. Draw a design on the paper, then tape it to the back of the glass. Following manufacturer's instructions, paint over the lines on the front of the glass with leading. Paint the design with glass paint.

3. Remove pattern and tape from glass. Secure glass in frames. Arrange and glue frames together.

Recycled items:
• two wooden frames with glass

You'll also need:
• acrylic primer
• acrylic paint
• paintbrushes
• clear acrylic sealer
• double-sided tape
• black liquid leading
• leading tips (optional)
• glass paints
• wood glue

Tip:
For a quick version of this project, use self-adhesive strips and circles of leading instead of drawing designs with liquid leading.

*Organize your
home office or even
your stationery stash
with a tasteful
triptych, tailor-made to match
your décor. With fabric-scrap pockets
and a covered cardboard base, it's a breeze to create!*

darling desk triptych

1. Enlarge the screen and hinge patterns on page 156 to the desired size. Use the patterns to cut one center and two side panels from cardboard (for the front panels) and one center and two side panels from poster board (for the back panels). Draw around one side panel four times and one center panel two times on fabric; cut out fabric pieces 1" outside of drawn lines. For hinges, fuse the wrong sides of two pieces of fabric together, then use the pattern to cut out two hinges.

2. Measure the width of the front center panel, then add 2". Cut one $4^1/_2$" and one $7^1/_2$" by the determined measurement pocket from fabric. Fuse the top edge of each pocket $1/_2$" to the wrong side. Matching side and bottom edges, stack short pocket on tall pocket, then stack pockets on front fabric panel, sew down center of pockets to secure them to the front panel.

3. Wrapping and gluing edges to the wrong side and clipping corners as needed, use spray adhesive to cover each cardboard and poster board piece with a fabric piece. Referring to Fig. 1 for placement, glue the hinges to the panels.

Fig. 1

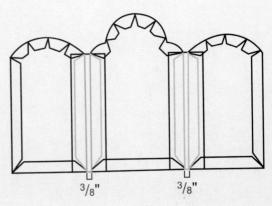

4. With wrong sides together, glue the front panels to the back panels. Glue cord along sides and top of screen.

5. For each decorative pushpin, glue one or more buttons to the top of a pushpin.

Recycled items:
- corrugated cardboard
- poster board or large gift boxes
- fabric remnants
- coordinating fabric-covered cord
- buttons
- clear plastic pushpins

You'll also need:
- paper-backed fusible web
- $1/_2$" wide fusible tape
- spray adhesive
- hot glue gun

eclectic mirror

Make a dramatic statement with this fashionable mirror. Contemporary colors and exotic styling are sure to fool your friends, but the "designer" mirror is actually enhanced with rolled newspaper "rays."

1. For the background, draw around the mirror on cardboard; cut out 1" outside drawn lines. Glue mirror to center of background.

2. For each tube, vertically roll half of a sheet of newspaper tightly around the dowel. Glue the edge to secure, then remove the dowel from the tube. Make enough tubes to cut the following lengths: forty-eight $1^1/_2$" lengths, four $2^1/_2$" lengths, sixteen $3^1/_4$" lengths, forty 6" lengths, and four 8" lengths. Cut out forty-four $^1/_2$" x $1^1/_2$" strips from newspaper for bands.

3. For the border strip, cut a 2" x 19" strip from newspaper. Fold strip in half lengthwise, then unfold; fold each long edge to the center, then

refold and glue strip in half lengthwise. Use 2" x 12" pieces of newspaper and repeat the process to make twelve more strips for curls.

4. Trim eight of the $3^1/_4$" and eight of the 6" tube ends at an angle. Prime, then paint the strips, the $1^1/_2$" tubes, the bands, and the plugs gold; prime, then paint all remaining tubes red.

5. Glue the border strip along the edge of the mirror. Glue bands around all of the 6" and 8" long tubes $3^1/_2$" from the bottom, then glue wood plugs into the tubes with straight ends. Referring to the diagram, page 150, arrange and glue tubes to the background. Curl remaining strips, then glue to the ends of the $2^1/_2$" tubes.

Recycled items:
• corrugated cardboard
• newspaper

You'll also need:
• 5" x 7" oval mirror
• craft glue
• $^1/_4$" diameter dowel
• spray primer
• gold and red spray paint
• eighty-four $^1/_4$" diameter
  wooden plugs

Spice up your kitchen curtains with creative tiebacks made from wooden spoons. Pretty polka dots, patterned bows, and eye-catching colors add a dash of fun.

stirring
curtain tiebacks

1. For each tieback, apply primer to spoon and one cardboard piece. Paint spoon as desired, then apply two coats of sealer.

2. Use pliers to bend two small zig-zags in one end of one wire (this holds the spoon in place). Keeping wire parallel with spoon handle, place zig-zags on back of spoon; staple one cardboard piece over zig-zags (Fig. 1). Bend wire into a hook shape, then make a curl in the remaining end.

Fig. 1

3. Tie ribbon into a bow around the tieback. Use a tack, screw, or nail through the curl to attach tieback to wall.

Recycled items:
- two wooden spoons
- two 1" x 1½" pieces of cardboard (we used a cereal box)
- two 13" long wire pieces from coat hangers
- ribbon

You'll also need:
- acrylic primer
- paintbrushes
- acrylic paints
- clear acrylic sealer
- pliers
- staple gun
- tacks, screws, or nails

Tip:
Use a new pencil eraser dipped in paint to make perfectly round dots!

Re-create the aura of an Old-World market with richly detailed "stone" carvings. Made with packing foam, newspaper, and fake fruit, these timeless plaques are truly a work of art.

"stone"
fruit plaques

Use modeling paste to attach pieces to foam. Allow the paste and sealer to dry after each application. More than one application of modeling paste and color wash may be necessary for desired effects.

1. For each plaque, cut one 5½" x 8½" plaque and one 1½" x 5½" trim piece from foam; glue the trim piece along the bottom front edge of the plaque. Round the top corners of the plaque, then scoop out an indention in the top back of the plaque for a hanger. Draw around the fruit on the plaque, then scoop out a depression inside the drawn lines to accommodate about half the thickness of the fruit piece.

2. Tear newspaper into 1" x 6" strips. Mix one part water with two parts glue. Saturate each strip in the glue mixture, then smooth strip onto front and sides of plaque. Glue fruit in the depression.

3. Cut a crack design in the plaque, then use a knife to push paste down into the crack. Cover the plaque with paste. Glue game pieces and letters to plaque, then cover them with a light layer of paste.

4. Paint the plaque as desired. Mix equal parts of stain, raw sienna paint, and antiquing glaze together for a wash. Apply wash to plaque; wipe plaque with a soft cloth to remove excess stain.

5. Apply two coats of sealer to plaque.

Recycled items:
- at least 1"-thick plastic foam
- plastic or foam fruit pieces
- newspaper
- flat round game pieces

You'll also need:
- tacky glue
- modeling paste
- ¾" tall self-adhesive three dimensional letters
- desired colors and raw sienna acrylic paints
- paintbrushes
- brown acrylic stain
- dark antiquing glaze
- clear acrylic sealer

Tip:
A serrated knife cuts and shapes foam easily, while a spoon is perfect to scoop out an indention.

painted
quilt-block rug

Finished in bold shades of red, white, and blue, this star-studded floor mat makes an inviting addition to your entryway. Create your own quilted rug with a bit of paint and leftover linoleum — no sewing skills required!

Allow gesso, paint, and sealer to dry after each application. Several coats of paint may be necessary for desired coverage.

1. Apply two coats of gesso to the wrong side of the vinyl piece. Draw a 3" wide border, then a 1½" wide border along the mat edges. Leaving 1½" between squares, draw six 6¾" squares inside the borders.

2. Trace the star design from page 151 onto tracing paper; transfer the design to each square. Referring to the photograph for color placement, paint the mat. Use the end of the paintbrush handle and the spouncer to add dots and the paint pen to draw V's and "stitches" on the designs as desired.

3. Trace the flower pattern from page 151 onto lid; cut out along the lines to make a stencil. Stencil flowers on the blue border. Use the spouncer to paint dots on the red border. Use the paint pen to outline the stenciled flowers,

draw swirls on the dots, and to draw X's on the blue border.

4. Apply three to four coats of sealer to mat.

Recycled items:
- 24" x 32¼" piece of vinyl floor covering
- clear plastic take-out food lid

You'll also need:
- white gesso
- tracing paper
- transfer paper
- light blue, blue, red, and white acrylic paint
- paintbrushes
- 1" diameter spouncer
- black paint pen
- clear acrylic spray sealer

"hip" message center

Faded jeans and a cardboard plaque make a lifesaving message center for students on the go. Co-eds, teens, and 'tweens can stuff the doorknob hanger's pocket with sticky notes for a cool way to touch base with family and friends.

1. Enlarge the pattern on page 152 by 143%; cut out pattern. Use the pattern to cut hanger from cardboard.

2. Draw around the hanger twice on the wrong side of denim. Cut out one piece (the back) along the drawn lines. Cut out the remaining piece (the front) ³/₄" outside the outer edge and ³/₄" inside the hole.

3. Clipping at ¹/₄" intervals to the drawn line, clip around the hole on the front denim piece. Wrapping and gluing edges to back, glue the front piece, then the back piece to the hanger.

4. Glue trim to the hanger. Arrange, then glue, pocket and loops to hanger; glue the ponytail holder around the hole and letters to spell a name at the top of the hanger.

Recycled items:
- corrugated cardboard
- denim jeans, a back pocket, and two belt loops
- beaded and fringed trim
- decorative ponytail holder

You'll also need:
- tacky glue
- 1" tall foam letters

photo bouquet

This picturesque bouquet has a sweet history — the pot is a plastic pudding cup, while the flowers are cut from an aluminum pan. Blooming with favorite photos, it makes a memorable accent for a side table or shelf.

1. Trace the flower pattern from page 149 onto tracing paper; cut out. For each flower, stick two magnets together. Use the adhesive sheet to adhere aluminum to the outsides of the magnets. Draw around pattern and make designs on the front of the flower; cut the flower out.

2. Paint stem green. Use welding compound to attach stem to back of flower.

3. Gluing edges to inside, cover cup with fabric; paint cup black. Spritz cup and excelsior with silver paint. Prepare enough plaster to almost fill cup; insert stems and allow to set. Glue excelsior to top of plaster; place photos between flower magnets.

Recycled items:
- advertiser's sheet magnets
- aluminum pan
- wire clothes hanger pieces for stems
- plastic pudding cup
- fabric remnant
- green excelsior
- photographs

You'll also need:
- tracing paper
- double-sided adhesive sheets
- green, black, and silver spray paint
- welding compound
- clear-drying household adhesive
- plaster of paris

dolled-up clock

Little glamour girls will adore our fun fashion clock. Adorned with a party mask, fancy hat, feather boa, and card stock curls, this trimmed-up timepiece is simply stunning.

Recycled items:
- wooden cigar box with hinged lid (ours measures 8³/₄" x 10")
- corrugated cardboard
- rigid plastic mask
- artificial eyelashes
- magazine
- lady's hat
- decorative braid
- feather boa

You'll also need:
- sandpaper
- tack cloth
- brown and desired "curl color" card stock
- tacky glue
- drill and drill bits
- clock kit with shaft to fit thickness of lid
- ³/₄" long nails
- acrylic primer and assorted paints
- paintbrushes
- four acrylic jewels
- iridescent glitter
- tape
- tracing paper
- gold paint pen
- craft crimper (for paper and lightweight metal)
- picture hanging kit

1. Remove the lid from the box. Remove paper from the box and lid; sand smooth and wipe with tack cloth.

2. Draw around the box once on the brown card stock and several times on cardboard; cut out the pieces $1/4$" inside the drawn lines. Stack and glue the cardboard pieces in the box to lessen the depth of the box. For the mask tab cover, draw around the mask at the center of the card stock piece; leaving outside intact, cut out $1/4$" inside lines.

3. Follow manufacturer's instructions to drill a hole for clock at center of lid. Glue, then nail the lid (smooth side up) onto the box (Fig. 1). Prime, then paint the box and lid the desired base coat color. Glue jewels to lid at the 3, 6, 9, and 12 o'clock positions. Using the photo as a guide, paint the clock face. Follow manufacturer's instructions to attach clock kit to the lid.

Fig. 1

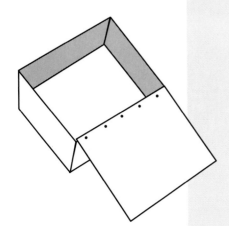

4. Apply primer, then base coat to the mask. Cut out eyes from the magazine to fit the mask; tape eyes in place on the backside of the mask. Paint details on the face as desired. Glue eyelashes in place. Glue glitter over "eye shadow." Make $1/2$" long cuts at $1/2$" intervals along the edges of the mask; bend clipped edges outward for tabs. Center and glue the mask in the box. Glue the mask tab cover around the mask.

5. Sizing to fit, copy, then cut out the hair background pattern from page 153. Use the pattern to cut hair background from cardboard. Paint background to blend with card stock for curls. Glue background to box.

6. Trace curl patterns, page 153, onto tracing paper; cut out. Use patterns to cut enough curls from card stock to cover the hair background. Draw gold highlights on the curls, then crimp them. Starting at the neckline, glue curls to background.

7. Cut hat in half; glue braid along cut edges. Glue hat to hair. Glue a piece of the boa to the hat for a band and under the chin for a scarf. Follow manufacturer's instructions to attach hanger to back of clock.

Tip:
If you can't find eyes to fit your mask in a magazine, select a pair you like, then size them on a color photocopier to fit the mask.

groovy showcase

Teens can show off favorite photos and tons of mementos in our trendy wall display.
The memory collage puts plenty of "trashy" objects to good use — fabric remnants,
assorted boxes, old scrunchies, even a scratched-up CD!

Recycled items:
- three large pieces of corrugated cardboard
- fabric remnants
- small cardboard boxes and lids
- decorative paper remnants
- hair scrunchies
- marabou boas
- assorted photographs
- assorted rubber stamps and ink pads, stickers, and magazines

You'll also need:
- tacky glue
- white poster board
- acrylic paint
- paintbrushes
- wire picture hanging kit

1. For board, cut four 24" squares of cardboard; stack and glue pieces together. Cover the board with poster board, then fabric.

2. Paint boxes and lids; line some of the boxes with paper. Glue boxes and lids to board.

3. Use scrunchies to make "flowers" and to trim some of the boxes. Glue boas along edges of board. Attach hanger to back of board.

4. Add assorted embellishments and photos to the board. Use rubber stamps, stickers, or letters from magazines to add captions to your photos.

> *Tip*
> To make CD photo frame, simply cut the background from a photo, then glue the photo to the CD...add stickers or paint designs around the photo.

kitty-cat
playground

This two-level tower is a feline wonderland! Plywood scraps, carpet remnants, and a mailing tube form a sturdy base, while colorful plastic lids, a toy ball, and a stuffed sock keep Kitty entertained.

1. Cut a 21" square base and a 13" x 21" top from plywood. Cut a 20" length from the mailing tube (column) and from the chair leg (post). Cut a 31" square and a 23" x 31" rectangle from carpet; measure around the column and add ¼", then cut a piece from carpet 20" long by the determined measurements.

2. Marking from corner to corner, draw an X on the base to find the center; use screws to attach one end of the post to the center of the base. Mark the center of the square piece of carpet; cut an X in the carpet at the center large enough to allow the carpet to slide down over the post. Apply glue to the top of the base; place the cut carpet piece on the base and smooth in place. Clipping corners as needed, wrap the carpet edges to the bottom of the base and staple in place.

3. Staple the 20" long piece of carpet around the column. Apply a thick layer of glue just inside the bottom of the column; place column over post. Fill column with sand or small pebbles.

4. For the sock dangle, fill the sock to the bottom of the cuff with fiberfill. Wrap and glue the rope in several smooth coils around the sock under the cuff, leaving the rope long enough to attach to the top of the tower and still dangle. Twist, then wrap and glue the cuff around the coils.

5. For the cap dangle, make a hole in the top of each cap. Leaving a long tail to attach to the top, thread rope, from outside to inside, through the hole in the bottom cap; knot the rope inside and just above the cap. Repeat to add remaining caps.

6. To attach each dangle, drill a hole on one short side of the tower top; thread the rope from the bottom through the hole and staple the end to the top. Glue the carpet rectangle to the top, clipping corners as needed; wrap, then staple the edges to the bottom. (Make a cut in the carpet to fit around the rope, if necessary.)

7. Determine the center of the tower top. Apply a thick bead of glue to the top of the column, then place the top on the column; use screws to attach the top to the post in the column.

8. For the spring-ball toy, twist one end of the spring through the carpet and staple the end in place. Twist the remaining end of wire through the ball several times.

Recycled items:
- large plywood remnants
- heavy-duty cardboard mailing tube
- 20" wooden table leg
- large carpet remnants
- wood screws
- sand or small pebbles
- child-size sock
- clothesline rope
- three colorful plastic caps (we used shaving gel caps)
- 1" diameter spiral from a notebook
- hollow or foam-core small ball

You'll also need:
- tacky glue
- heavy-duty staple gun
- polyester fiberfill
- drill and bits

whimsical delights for the porch and yard

garden
fresh

Whip up whimsical delights for the porch and yard with a plethora of household "trash." Make a delightful plant stand from stools and coffee cans. Transform an old tin canister into a ladybug birdhouse. Adorn your plants with sparkling hair-clip butterflies, or enhance your garden trellis with precocious bottle bugs. What fun!

1. Measure across the widest part of the gelatin container, then subtract 2"; cut three lengths of wire the determined measurements. Twist the wires together at the center, then spread ends apart evenly.

2. For body, cut 4" lengths of driftwood for the head, tail, and legs; cut one end of each piece at a 45° angle. Drill a small hole in the straight end of each piece, then fill the holes with glue; slide one wood piece onto each wire end (Fig. 1).

Fig. 1

3. Place container on body; mark, then notch container to accommodate about one-third of the thickness of each wooden piece.

4. Mix concrete. Place container on a flat surface, then place body on container. Fill container with concrete, being sure to cover wires completely by slightly mounding concrete over center of body. Allow concrete to harden, then remove from container.

5. Paint the turtle shell green; head, tail, legs, and clam shells light green; and the bubble shells white. *Sponge Paint* light green squares around the turtle shell, then outline them black; add green dots to the legs, neck, and tail and a black iris with a white highlight to each bubble shell for eyes.

6. To assemble eyes, glue the bubble shells to the head, then the clam shells to the bubble shells for eyelids.

7. Apply two coats of sealer to turtle.

Recycled items:
- family-size plastic gelatin container
- 1" diameter pieces of driftwood
- two clam shells
- two bubble shells

You'll also need:
- wire cutters
- craft wire
- saw and miter box
- drill and bits
- wood glue
- ready-to-mix concrete
- green, light green, white, and black acrylic paint
- paintbrushes
- small rectangle of sponge
- clear-drying household cement
- clear exterior grade matte sealer

Craft Technique:
- *Sponge Painting*, page 158

terrace turtle

This winsome garden turtle is a simply delightful deck decoration. Mold his body by pouring concrete into a gelatin container. A trip to the beach will provide you with the rest of your materials — shells for his eyes and driftwood for his head, tail, and legs!

glittering butterflies

Delight your children or your inner child with dazzling plastic butterflies in a rainbow of colors. A hair-clip body makes it easy to attach these shimmering creatures to bushes, hedges, climbing plants, and more.

1. Use a photocopier to size the patterns from page 155 to fit your clips, then cut them out. (For our large butterfly, we used a $3^1/2$" long clip and used the pattern as is. For our smaller butterflies, we used $2^1/2$" long clips and photocopied the pattern at 77% to reduce it.)

2. For each butterfly, using the patterns, cut four large borders (blue) and four small borders (yellow) from the lids. For wing centers, draw around the outside edge of each border pattern twice on plastic sheets; cut out each piece $1/4$" inside the drawn lines.

3. Allowing to dry after each application, apply two coats of paint to both sides of each border and center piece…sprinkle glitter onto each piece while second coat of paint is still wet.

4. For each wing, glue the edges of the center piece between two border pieces. Punch two holes near the flat edge of each wing. Wire wings to hair clips.

5. Cut two 6" lengths of wire. For each antennae, thread a bead onto center of one wire, then fold wire in half; leaving $1/2$" at each end straight, twist wires to "spiral" antennae. Use the straight wires to secure antennae to the hair clip.

Recycled items:
- plastic spring-type hair clips
- large plastic lids
- heavy-duty plastic sheet protectors
- pony beads

You'll also need:
- spray paint for plastic
- micro glitter
- clear-drying all-weather adhesive
- $1/16$" diameter hole punch
- black craft wire
- wire cutters

If you're looking for a fresh way to display your favorite flowers, our distinctive plant stand really stacks up! Wooden stools provide plenty of rungs for hanging coffee can planters, and cheerful spring colors complete the effect.

tiptop plant stand

Allow wood filler, primer, paint, and sealer to dry after each application.

1. For stand, clamp stools seats together. Drilling a pilot hole first and twisting screw heads below the surface of the top seat, use screws to attach stools together. Spread wood filler over the heads; sand areas smooth and wipe with the tack cloth.

2. Apply white primer, then base coat to stand. Using tape to mask evenly spaced areas, paint checkerboard stripes along the seat edges and rings around the rungs. Use the eraser to paint dot flowers on the legs, then freehand stems and leaves.

3. For each can planter, drill drainage holes in bottom can and holes below rim on opposite sides of the can for hangers. Measure the length the planter needs to hang from the rung and add 5"; cut two lengths from coat hanger wire the determined measurement. Thread 2" of one wire through one hanger hole; wrap wire around itself to secure. Bend remaining end into a hook shape. Repeat for the other side of the can.

4. Apply rust-colored primer, then a white base coat to planter. Apply two coats of desired color topcoat to planter. Lightly sand planter to create an aged look, then wipe with the tack cloth.

5. To paint flowers on the planter, pour a thin layer of paint for petals on one plate and color for centers on other plate. Wad a bag into a tight ball. Dip the ball into the petal paint, then dab onto the planter. Paint the petals, then the centers.

6. Apply sealer to stools and planters. Plant flowers in each planter, then hang from stand.

Recycled items:
- two identical wooden stools
- tin cans for planters
- lightweight coat hangers
- two plastic foam plates
- small plastic grocery bags

You'll also need:
- C-clamps
- drill and bits
- wood screws $1\frac{1}{2}$-times longer than thickness of one stool seat
- wood filler
- sandpaper and tack cloth
- white and rust-colored spray primers
- white and assorted colors of acrylic paints
- paintbrushes
- painter's masking tape
- pencil with new eraser
- wire cutters
- clear acrylic spray sealer

backyard
bottle bugs

Add a touch of whimsy to your trellis, fence, or garden wall with this trio of mischievous hanging bugs. The colorful critters are made from empty soda bottles, plastic "prize" containers, and spiral notebook wire. How clever!

1. For each bug, trim the neck of one bottle (body) until the cap of the prize container (head) fits into the opening. For feet, punch a hole through the center of six bottle caps. Cut six 2½" lengths of coils for legs and two 2" lengths of coils for antennae from coiled notebook spirals.

2. Prime feet, legs, and antennae. Use acrylic paint to paint the feet and add dots. Spray paint the legs, antennae, head, and body.

3. Insert the head into the body, then mark placement for antennae on body at edge of head; remove head. Use pushpin to punch holes for antennae, legs (at bottom of body), and hanger (at top of body). Cut a 1" long slot in top of body for wings.

4. For the hanger, thread the ends of a length of fishing line through the button; knot ends together. Thread hanger loop through hole (from inside body out). Glue button to inside of body.

5. To attach each leg, twist one end of one leg through the hole in one foot; coil wire flat against bottom of foot. Twist top of leg two or three times through a leg hole in the body. Glue to inside of body.

6. For wings, push ends of leaves through slot in body; arrange as desired and glue ends to inside of body.

7. For each antenna, stretch one antenna coil and glue a bead onto one end. Thread opposite end through hole for antennae, bend against inside of body and glue in place.

8. For eyes, coiling wire above and below bead to secure it in place, attach one bead to each end of a 12" length of wire. Remove cap from head. Fold wire in half; place fold in wire inside the head, then replace cap. Glue head to body. Draw a big smile on the bug.

Recycled items:
- 16-ounce plastic beverage bottles
- plastic prize containers from toy-vending machines
- nail
- metal bottle caps
- wire spirals from notebooks
- buttons
- leaves from silk flowers
- assorted beads

You'll also need:
- spray acrylic primer
- assorted acrylic paints for feet
- paintbrushes
- assorted colors spray paint for plastic
- pushpin
- fishing line
- hot glue gun
- craft wire
- black permanent marker

guardian
garden angel

1. For the stand, refer to Fig. 1a to cut away the wire on the tomato cage as indicated in red. Stand will look like Fig. 1b. Stretch the end uprights apart to fit along the second and fourth slats on the trellis (body), then craft wire them in place with the points extending past the bottom of the trellis for ground stakes (Fig. 2a and 2b).

Fig. 1a   **Fig. 1b**

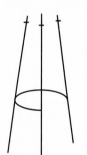

Fig. 2a   **Fig. 2b**

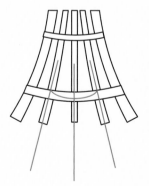

2. Glue wood pieces to back bottom of lid (head); glue head to body. Drill two holes across each end of each handle (arms). Crisscrossing the arms so they naturally curve around in front of the body; overlap one end of each arm at back of body about 6" below the head, then tack in place. Prime, then paint the body, stand, head, and arms white.

3. Cut the hook from two hangers (twisted parts of hangers are the ends). For each wing, form hanger into a wing-shape. Stretch one leg of hosiery over hanger and gather around the wire end; wrap craft wire around gathers to secure. Trim excess hosiery. Staple, then glue wings to back of body over ends of arms.

4. For wreath, cut the hook and twisted part from the remaining hanger. Make a hook at each end of wire, then hook ends together for the wreath base. Use craft wire to attach greenery and garland to the base; glue and/or wire flowers to wreath. Craft wire wreath to ends of arms through drilled holes.

5. Glue flowers to head for halo. Glue hardware piece to front of body under "chin."

With her trellis dress and wire hanger wings, this garden statue looks heavenly in any al fresco location. She's simply divine as the focal point of a flowerbed, yet lovely enough to stand on her own.

Recycled items:
- standard-size wire tomato cage
- wooden fan trellis
- small pieces of wood or wooden game pieces
- metal cookie tin lid
- two handles from wooden market baskets
- three metal clothes hangers
- two legs from white hosiery
- artificial greenery, garlands, and flowers
- decorative hardware piece

You'll also need:
- wire cutters
- craft wire
- clear-drying all-weather adhesive
- drill and bits
- upholstery tacks
- spray primer
- white spray paint
- staple gun

ladybug
birdhouse

A hospitable home for feathered friends, this lively little ladybug is just the thing to add a "spot" of color to the porch or garden. Create the lighthearted birdhouse with a cookie tin, soda cans, and a few odds and ends from your craft closet.

1. Draw a circle near the edge on the top of the lid for the birdhouse opening. Drill a hole through the center of the circle large enough to accommodate the point of scissors. Cut clips from center hole to drawn line like cutting a pie; trim points to $1/4$" long tabs. Bend tabs to inside of lid.

2. For perch, drill a hole 1" below opening to accommodate the bolt. Thread end of bolt through hole and twist nut onto bolt inside lid; glue nut in place.

3. To make the head, arrange the lid on the end cap to mark desired size for head; draw on cap along lid, then cut out along drawn line. Place lid on tin and turn tin on its side. Place head on edge of lid; mark holes on tin just under lid and in head for antennae. Remove lid and head; drill holes. Drill two holes at the top back of the tin for the hanger.

4. Cut through openings and down sides of cans to bottom rims. Cut away and discard tops and bottoms of cans; flatten remaining pieces. Size the wing pattern on page 152 to fit lid. Use pattern to cut two wings from can pieces.

5. Apply primer to lid, tin, head, antennae, and wings. Spray paint lid, tin, head and antennae black and wings red. Use acrylic paint to make black dots on wings.

Tip:
If the can pieces aren't large enough to cut your wings from, you can use a disposable aluminum baking sheet.

6. For the hanger, thread ends of a length of wire through holes in tin; twist wires together inside the tin to secure. Place lid on tin. Glue head and wings to lid. Thread one end of each antennae through holes in tin; bend ends flat to inside of tin and glue in place. Thread ends of antennae through holes in head and curl the ends.

7. Apply two coats of sealer to birdhouse.

Recycled items:
- metal cookie tin with lid
- bolt and nut
- plastic end cap from mailing tube
- two 4" long plastic-coated twist ties for antennae
- two aluminum beverage cans
- metal washer

You'll also need:
- utility scissors
- drill and bits
- clear-drying household cement
- spray primer
- black and red spray paint
- black acrylic paint
- paintbrush
- clear spray acrylic sealer

1. For the vase and handles, mark around one bottle 7" and 7½" from the bottom; cut along the marks, then discard the top of the bottle. Cut the ½" wide strip into two 9" lengths for the handles; discard the remainder of the strip. Cut out the smooth center sections of the remaining bottles (between horizontal ridges, if applicable), discarding the tops and bottoms of the bottles.

2. Cut each center section open down one side; cutting from short edge to short edge, cut the sections into 1" wide strips. From the strips, cut seven 18½" long base strips and fifteen 9" long strips. Score each 9" strip 1" from each end.

3. Referring to Fig. 1, place the base strips (white strips) side-by-side horizontally on a flat surface; tape across the strips. Moving tape as needed to hold strips in place, starting and ending with 9" strips (grey) flush with ends of base strips, and evenly spacing remaining strips in between end strips, weave 9" strips through the base strips. Cut strips along scored lines; fold remaining long ends to back and tape in place. Punch holes through all layers in the center of each "square" along the short edges.

Fig. 1

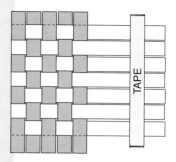

4. Tape the woven piece around the vase, then use ribbon to lace the edges together shoelace-style.

5. Punch holes in the vase along the top edge at front and back to attach handles. Punch evenly spaced holes lengthwise down the center of each handle. Weave ribbon through the holes, then tape to secure. Use earrings to attach handles to the front and fasteners to attach handles to the back of the vase.

Recycled items:
- four white gallon-size plastic bottles
- post-style dangle earrings with backs

You'll also need:
- utility scissors
- white duct tape
- craft knife and cutting mat
- ⅛" diameter hole punch
- 3⅓ yards narrow ribbon
- two brass paper fasteners

basket-weave
planter

Give your favorite potted plant a
feminine flourish! Woven from
four bleach bottles, this beribboned
"basket" is a dainty addition to a
patio table. Cast-off earrings add
extra sparkle.

Patio Birdcage

Recycled items:
- artificial greenery
- clear decorative miniature lights
- wire birdcage
- sheer fabric curtain (reserve an 18" x 20" piece for rosette)
- long sheer embossed scarf
- rubber bands
- ribbon
- decorative pearl hair clip
- artificial greenery garland

You'll also need:
- craft wire
- hot glue gun
- two decorative doves

1. Using wire to secure in place as needed, arrange greenery and lights inside cage, being sure the plug is placed at the top back of the cage.

2. Gathering underneath, drape cage with curtain and scarf; secure gathers with rubber bands. Tie ribbon into a bow around the gathers.

3. For the rosette, overlap the short ends of the reserved piece of curtain until the piece is 7" wide. Baste fabric lengthwise; pull threads to gather into a rosette. Stitch rosette to bottom front of cage, then attach the hair clip to the rosette center. Drape, then tack, the garland across the cage. Glue the doves to the top of the cage.

captivating wedding showpiece

Honor the bride and groom with an enchanting wedding decoration. Covered with sheer fabric scraps and illuminated by white Christmas lights, an old birdcage brings vintage elegance to the happy occasion, while plastic bottles make delightful light covers.

Floral Light Cover Garland

1. For each light cover, drill a hole through the center of the bottle cap to fit over lightbulb socket. Cut a wavy edge around bottle about 1" below bottom of cap; discard bottom of bottle. Apply primer, then paint light covers.

2. For each flower petal, cut one 12" length of wire; shape the wire to form a petal, then twist the ends together. Cut a 5" x 7" piece from hosiery. Smooth the hosiery over the petal, gathering the ends around the twisted wire; wrap wire around gathers to secure in place. Arrange ends of petals around the light cover cap; catching sprigs of greenery in with the gathers, wrap a piece of wire, then tape around cap to secure. Trim excess wire and hosiery ends.

3. Gathering the curtain lengthwise, wrap the lights, greenery, and beads around the curtain to form garland. Wrap garland around a post to cover wiring from the Patio Birdcage; tack in place as needed.

Recycled items:
- 12-ounce plastic beverage bottles with caps
- clear miniature decorative lights
- white hosiery
- white sheer curtains
- sprigs and garlands of artificial greenery
- long lengths of pearl-like beads

You'll also need:
- drill and bits
- utility scissors
- white spray primer
- cream-colored spray paint for plastic
- 20-gauge craft wire
- wire cutters
- white tape

handbag house plate

For the prettiest house sign on the block, fill a straw purse with fresh or artificial flowers. Hide beverage containers full of water in the handbag to keep cut flowers hydrated.

Recycled items:
- two colors of yarn remnants
- straw purse with handles
- large plastic lids (ours came from coffee cans)
- white and yellow plastic shopping or newspaper bags
- artificial leaves
- plastic containers to fit in purse (optional)
- silk flowers (optional)

You'll also need:
- tacky glue
- spray paint for plastic
- fresh-cut flowers (optional)

1. Alternating colors and gluing ends to secure, wrap yarn lengths around the purse handles to create stripes.

2. Draw numbers on the lids; cut out. Paint the numbers, then glue them to the front of the purse.

3. For each flower on the purse, cut five 1¹⁄₂" x 8" white strips and one 1" x 6" yellow strip from the bags. For each petal, fold the long edges of one white strip to the center, then fold strip in half lengthwise; fold ends to the center. Stack the petals together. For flower center, fold the yellow strip in half lengthwise, then tie it around the center of the white stack; fluff petals. Glue flower and a leaf to the purse.

4. If using fresh-cut flowers, cut the tops from containers, fill them with water and flowers and place in purse…or, arrange silk flowers in the purse. Hang purse near front door on porch.

precious trellis planter

Lush greenery climbs a "trellis" made of a flat sewing trim spool, giving this miniature flower box the air of a fairy tale cottage.

Recycled items:
- plastic diaper wipes container with lid
- square piece of sponge
- plastic spool from fringe or trim

You'll also need:
- acrylic primer
- white spray paint for plastic
- acrylic paint for stripe
- all-over print napkins
- découpage glue
- awl and hammer
- craft wire and wire cutters

Crafting Techniques:
- *Sponge Painting, page 158*
- *Découpage, page 157*

1. Carefully remove the lid from the container. Prime, then paint container and lid white. *Sponge Paint* a checkerboard stripe along the lip of the container.

2. Separate the plies of napkins. Starting under the rim, *Découpage* the printed napkin layers to the container.

3. Punch drainage holes in the bottom of the container. Punch holes in the back of the container as needed to wire the spool to the container for the trellis.

143

garden girl

1. Referring to Fig. 1, cut two hair pieces (red), one skirt piece (blue), and one arm piece (green) from coat hangers.

Fig. 1

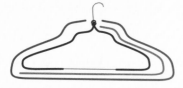

2. Refer to the diagram below to shape the hair and skirt pieces (make a small hook-shape at each wire end in the skirt "hem" to hook the skirt together). Curl each end of the arm piece around the jar about 1¹⁄₂ times. Use wire to attach the pieces together where indicated by X's...wrap wire around the pieces several times.

Diagram

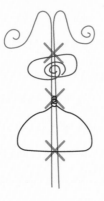

3. Apply primer to girl and jewelry pieces; paint girl white and jewelry yellow. Wrap a length of wire around girl where each piece of jewelry is to go. Following manufacturer's instructions, use putty to attach jewelry pieces to hair, neck, waist, and along skirt hem to conceal the wired areas.

4. Using wax crystals and a wick, follow manufacturer's instructions to make a candle in the jar.

Recycled items:
- lightweight metal coat hangers
- small jar for candleholder
- large metal jewelry pieces

You'll also need:
- wire cutters
- pliers
- 20-gauge wire
- spray primer
- white and yellow spray paint
- epoxy putty
- wax crystals and a wick

Why pay for an expensive garden sculpture when you can create your own with coat hangers, metal jewelry, and a bit of paint? This delightful candle-bearer is simple to make and oh-so enchanting!

stepping stone clock

1. Remove hardware from door. Sand the door, then wipe it with the tack cloth. Apply primer, then dark grey spray paint to the door.

2. Cut out a 7" diameter circle and assorted sizes of "stones" from the wooden crates to fit on the door. Use textured paint to paint the circle green and the stones grey (more than one coat of paint may be necessary).

3. Trace the verse design from page 154 onto tracing paper; transfer the design to the circle. Use non-textured paints to paint the design. Outline the design with the marker. Arrange and glue center and stones on door.

4. Trace the tool patterns from page 154 onto tracing paper and cut out. Place patterns on curved parts of bowl like the tools would naturally curve. Draw around the patterns, then cut out along drawn lines. Spray tools black.

5. Attach picture hangers to top back of door. Follow manufacturer's instructions to drill a hole through the center of the circle and to install the clock. Glue the tool pieces to the end of the clock hands.

Recycled items:
- wooden cabinet door
- wooden vegetable crates or baskets
- plastic butter bowl

You'll also need:
- sandpaper
- tack cloth
- spray primer
- dark grey spray paint
- utility scissors
- green and grey textured patio paint
- paintbrushes
- tracing paper
- transfer paper
- assorted colors of non-textured patio paints
- black permanent marker
- clear-drying household cement
- black spray paint for plastic
- picture hanging kit
- drill and bits
- clock kit with black hands and shaft to accommodate thickness of door

Anytime is time for gardening!

Time may fly when you're having fun, but at least you can keep track of hours spent in the garden with this clever cabinet-door clock. Textured wooden "stones" and garden tool clock hands (cut from a plastic container) add an earthy touch.

Playful Paper Bouquet
(page 65)

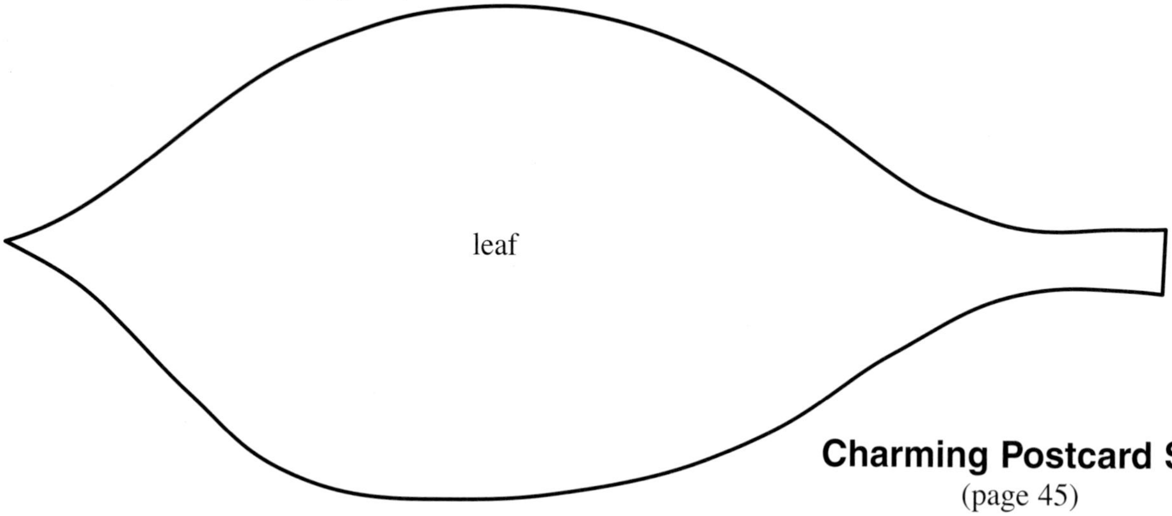

leaf

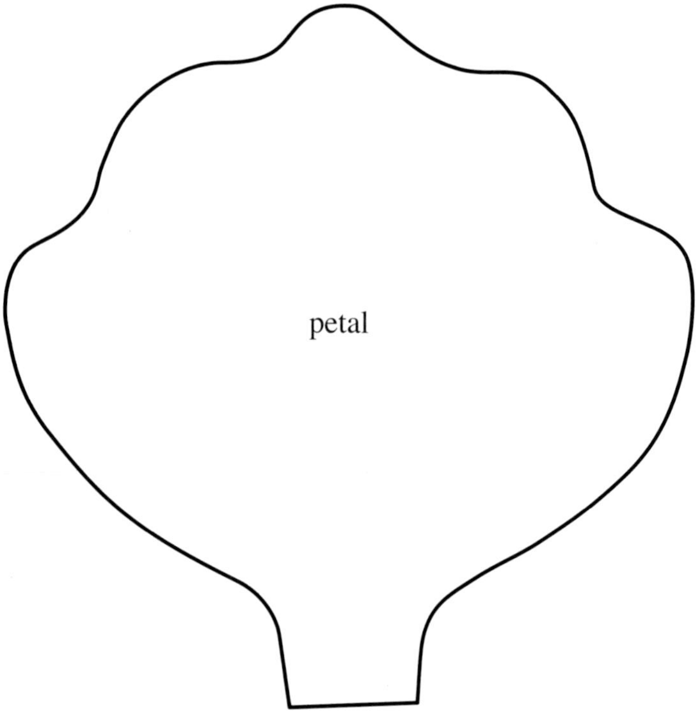

Charming Postcard Set
(page 45)

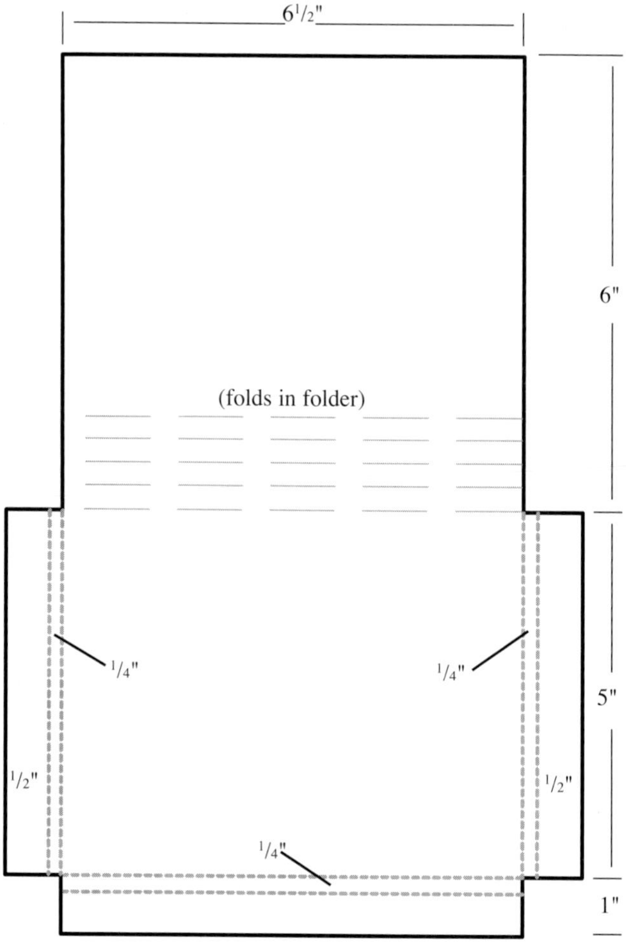

6¹/₂"

6"

(folds in folder)

¹/₄"   ¹/₄"

5"

¹/₂"   ¹/₂"

¹/₄"

1"

petal

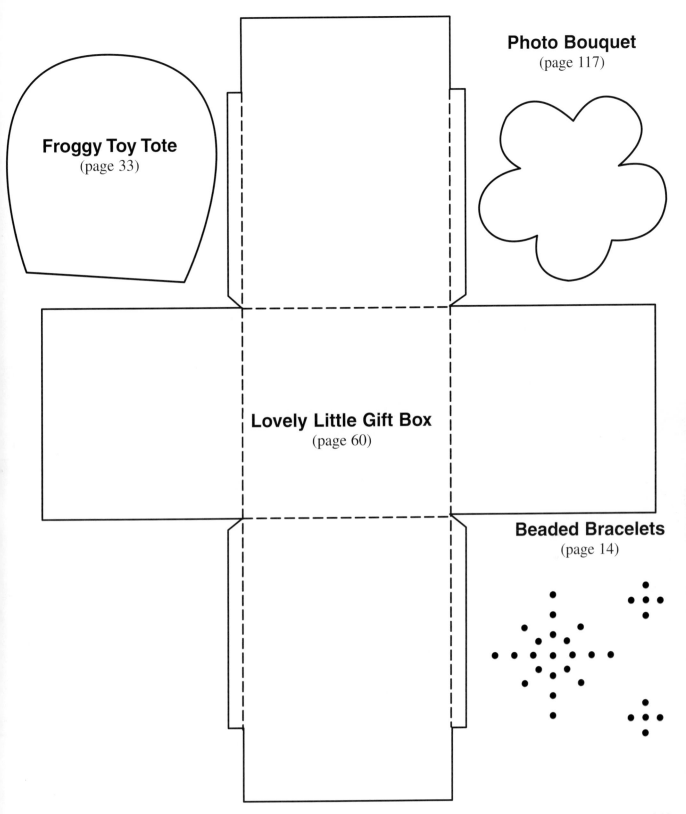

Froggy Toy Tote
(page 33)

Photo Bouquet
(page 117)

Lovely Little Gift Box
(page 60)

Beaded Bracelets
(page 14)

149

Eclectic Mirror
(page 109)

Assembly Diagram

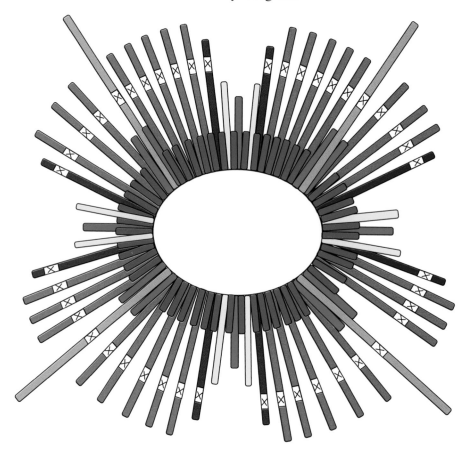

■	12	3" tubes
☐	8	4" tubes
■	8	5^1/$_2$" tubes
■	32	6" tubes
☐	4	8" tubes
■	48	1^1/$_2$" tubes
⊠	44	^{1}/$_2$" x ^{1}/$_2$" bands

Painted Quilt-Block Rug

(page 115)

"Hip" Message Center
(page 116)

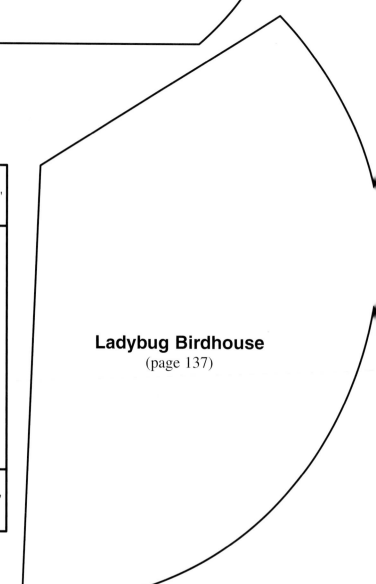

Vintage Patchwork Throw
(page 82)

Assembly Diagram

13" x 13"	9" x 37"		13" x 13"
	5" x 37"		

		13" x 13"	13" x 13"	13" x 13"		
9" x 49"	5" x 49"	13" x 13"	13" x 13"	13" x 13"	5" x 49"	9" x 49"
		13" x 13"	13" x 13"	13" x 13"		
		13" x 13"	13" x 13"	13" x 13"		

13" x 13"	5" x 37"		13" x 13"
	9" x 37"		

Ladybug Birdhouse
(page 137)

Dolled-Up Clock
(page 119)

Anytime is time for gardening!

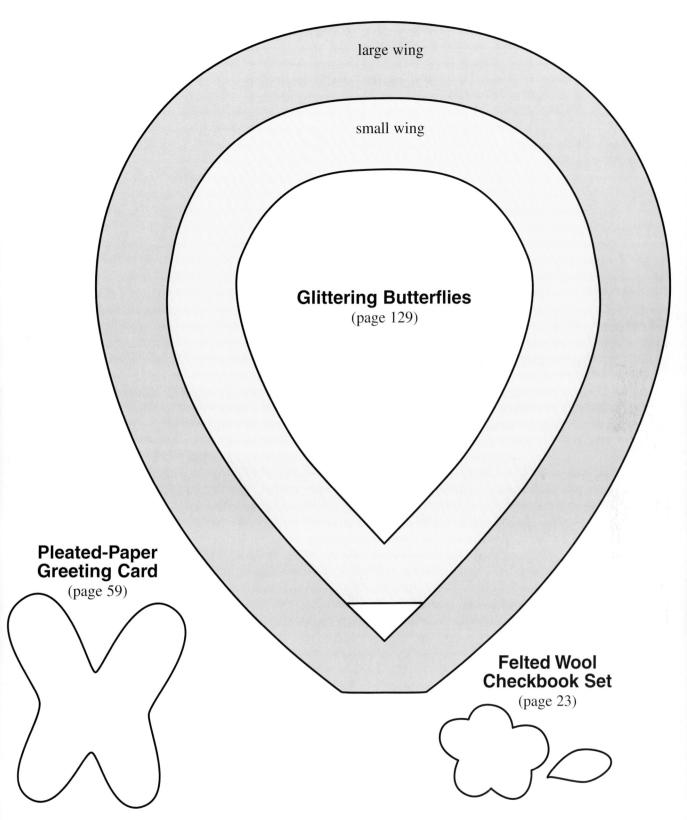

large wing

small wing

Glittering Butterflies
(page 129)

**Pleated-Paper
Greeting Card**
(page 59)

**Felted Wool
Checkbook Set**
(page 23)

Darling Desk Triptych

(page 107)

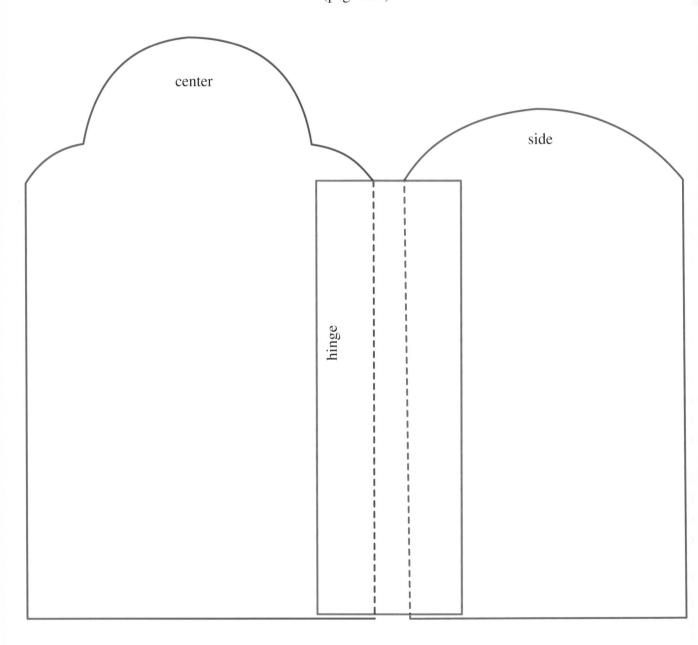

center

side

hinge

general instructions

ADHESIVES

When using any adhesive, carefully follow the manufacturer's instructions.

Craft glue stick: Recommended for paper or for gluing small, lightweight items to paper or other surfaces. Dry flat.

Découpage glue: Recommended for découpaging fabric or paper to a surface such as wood or glass. Use purchased découpage glue or mix one part craft glue with one part water.

Fabric glue: Recommended for fabric or paper. Dry flat or secure items with clothespins or straight pins until glue is dry.

Hot or low-temperature glue gun: Recommended for paper, fabric, florals, or wood. Hold in place until set.

Household cement: Recommended for ceramic or metal. Secure items with clothespins until glue is dry.

Rubber cement: Recommended for paper and cardboard. May discolor photos; may discolor paper with age. Dry flat (dries very quickly).

Spray adhesive: Recommended for paper or fabric. Can be repositioned or permanent. Dry flat.

Silicone adhesive: Recommended for ceramic, glass, leather, rubber, wood, and plastics. Forms a flexible and waterproof bond.

Tacky craft glue: Recommended for paper, fabric, florals, or wood. Dry flat or secure items with clothespins or straight pins until glue is dry.

White craft glue: Recommended for paper. Dry flat.

Wood glue: Recommended for wood. Nail, screw, or clamp items together until glue is dry.

DÉCOUPAGE

1. Cut desired motifs from fabric or paper.

2. Apply découpage glue to wrong sides of motifs.

3. Arrange motifs on project as desired, overlapping as necessary. Smooth in place and allow to dry.

4. Allowing to dry after each application, apply two to three coats of sealer to project.

PAINTING TECHNIQUES

TRANSFERRING A PATTERN

Trace pattern onto tracing paper. Place transfer paper, coated side down, between project and traced pattern. Use removable tape to secure pattern to project. Use a pencil to transfer outlines of design to project (press lightly to avoid smudges and heavy lines that are difficult to cover). If necessary, use a soft eraser to remove any smudges.

TRANSFERRING DETAILS

To transfer detail lines to design, position transfer paper and pattern over painted basecoat and use pencil to lightly transfer detail lines onto project.

ADDING DETAILS

Use a permanent marker or paint pen (usually with a fine-tip) to draw over transferred detail lines or to create freehand details on project.

PAINTING BASE COATS

A base coat is a solid color of paint that covers the project's entire surface.

Use a medium round brush for large areas and a small round brush for small areas. Do not overload brush. Allowing to dry after each application, apply several thin coats of paint to project.

DRY BRUSH

This technique creates a random coloration that sits on top of the project's surface. It is similar to a color wash, yet creates an aged look.

Do not dip brush in water. Dip a stipple brush or old paintbrush in paint; wipe most of the paint off onto a dry paper towel. Lightly rub the brush across the area to receive color. Decrease pressure on the brush as you move outward. Repeat as needed to create the desired coverage of color.

HIGHLIGHTING AND SHADING

To side load brush, dip one corner of a flat brush in water; blot on a paper towel. Dip dry corner of brush into paint. Stroke brush back and forth on palette until there is a gradual change from paint to water in each brush stroke. Stroke loaded side of brush along detail line on project, pulling brush toward you and turning project if necessary. For highlighting, side load brush with a lighter color of paint. For shading, side load brush with a darker color of paint.

SPATTER PAINTING

Dip the bristle tips of a dry toothbrush into paint, blot on a paper towel to remove excess, then pull thumb across bristles to spatter paint on project.

SPONGE PAINTING

1. Dampen sponge with water.
2. Dip dampened sponge into paint; blot on paper towel to remove excess paint.
3. Use a light stamping motion to paint project. Allow to dry.
4. If using more than one color of paint, repeat Steps 1 – 3, using a fresh sponge piece for each color.
5. If desired, repeat technique using one color again over areas of other colors, to soften edges or to lighten up a heavy application of one color.

STENCILING

To make a stencil, cut a piece of clear plastic lid at least 1" larger on all sides than pattern. Place plastic directly over pattern in book. Use a fine-point permanent marker to trace pattern. Place plastic on cutting mat and use craft knife to cut out design sections, making sure plastic edges are smooth.
Pour a small amount of paint onto a paper plate. Hold or tape (using removable tape) stencil in place on project. Dip a stencil brush or sponge piece in paint and remove excess on a paper towel. Working from edges of cut out areas toward center, apply paint in a stamping motion. Carefully lift stencil from project. To stencil a design in reverse, clean stencil and turn stencil over.

MAKING PATTERNS

Place tracing paper over pattern and trace lines of pattern; cut out.

For a more durable pattern, use a permanent pen to trace pattern onto stencil plastic instead of tracing paper. Or cut out the tracing paper pattern, place it on cardboard, draw around it, and then cut out a cardboard pattern.

When only a half pattern is shown (indicated by a solid blue line on pattern), fold tracing paper in half. Place the fold along solid blue line and trace pattern half. Turn paper over and draw along pattern half. Open tracing paper and cut out whole pattern.

EMBROIDERY STITCHES
BLANKET STITCH

Bring needle up at 1; keeping thread below point of needle, go down at 2 and up at 3 (Fig. 1a). Continue working as shown in Fig. 1b.

Fig. 1a   Fig. 1b

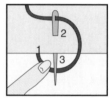

RUNNING STITCH

Make a series of straight stitches with stitch length equal to the space between stitches (Fig. 2).

Fig. 2

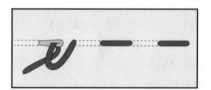

credits

We want to extend a warm thank you to the generous people who allowed us to photograph our projects at their homes: Tommy and Donna Harkins, Patti Kymer, Tim and Janna Laughlin, Vicki Moody, Ellison Poe, and Sam and Karen Welch.

A special thanks goes to Husqvarna Viking Sewing Machine Company of Cleveland, Ohio, for providing the sewing machines used to create several of our projects. We also extend our gratitude to the following companies for providing us with their fine products: Beacon Chemical Company of Mount Vernon, New York, and Therm O Web of Wheeling, Illinois.

To photographers Jerry R. Davis of Jerry Davis Photography and Ken West of Ken West Photography, both of Little Rock, Arkansas, we say thank you for your time, patience, and excellent work.

Our sincere appreciation goes to Neal Lea for her modeling contributions to this book.